T0316594

Cambridge Elements ≡

Elements in Earth System Governance
edited by
Frank Biermann
Utrecht University
Aarti Gupta
Wageningen University
Michael Mason
London School of Economics and Political Science (LSE)

ADAPTIVE GOVERNANCE TO MANAGE HUMAN MOBILITY AND NATURAL RESOURCE STRESS

Saleem H. Ali
University of Delaware

Martin Clifford
University of Delaware

Dominic Kniveton
University of Sussex

Caroline Zickgraf
University of Liège

Sonja Ayeb-Karlsson
University College London and United Nations University Institute for Environment and Human Security

CAMBRIDGE
UNIVERSITY PRESS

CAMBRIDGE
UNIVERSITY PRESS

Shaftesbury Road, Cambridge CB2 8EA, United Kingdom

One Liberty Plaza, 20th Floor, New York, NY 10006, USA

477 Williamstown Road, Port Melbourne, VIC 3207, Australia

314–321, 3rd Floor, Plot 3, Splendor Forum, Jasola District Centre, New Delhi – 110025, India

103 Penang Road, #05–06/07, Visioncrest Commercial, Singapore 238467

Cambridge University Press is part of Cambridge University Press & Assessment, a department of the University of Cambridge.

We share the University's mission to contribute to society through the pursuit of education, learning and research at the highest international levels of excellence.

www.cambridge.org
Information on this title: www.cambridge.org/9781009357722
DOI: 10.1017/9781009357708

First published 2023

A catalogue record for this publication is available from the British Library.

ISBN 978-1-009-35772-2 Paperback
ISSN 2631-7818 (online)
ISSN 2631-780X (print)

Cambridge University Press & Assessment has no responsibility for the persistence or accuracy of URLs for external or third-party internet websites referred to in this publication and does not guarantee that any content on such websites is, or will remain, accurate or appropriate.

Adaptive Governance to Manage Human Mobility and Natural Resource Stress

Elements in Earth System Governance

DOI: 10.1017/9781009357708
First published online: January 2023

Saleem H. Ali
University of Delaware

Martin Clifford
University of Delaware

Dominic Kniveton
University of Sussex

Caroline Zickgraf
University of Liège

Sonja Ayeb-Karlsson
University College London and United Nations University Institute for Environment and Human Security

Author for correspondence: Saleem H. Ali, Saleem@udel.edu

Abstract: Connections between resources and migration operate as a complex adaptive system rather than being premised in linear, causal mechanisms. The systems thinking advocated within this Element increases the inclusion of socio-psychological, financial, demographic, environmental, and political dimensions that mediate resource-(im) mobility pathways. The Earth Systems Governance (ESG) paradigm provides a way to manage global migration flows more effectively, allowing for consideration of networks and interdependencies in addition to its inherent adaptiveness. Resource rushes, hydropower displacement, and climate-induced retreat from coastal areas are all examples of circumstances linking resources and human mobility. Movement can also ameliorate environmental conditions, and hence close monitoring of impacts and policies that harness benefits of migration is advocated. Green remittance bonds, and land tenure policies favouring better arable resource usage are key ingredients of a more systems-oriented approach to managing mobility. The Global Compact for Migration offers an opportunity to operationalize such adaptive governance approaches in the Anthropocene.

Keywords: migration, global environmental change, resource security, environmental peacebuilding, human mobility

ISBNs: 9781009357722 (PB), 9781009357708 (OC)
ISSNs: 2631-7818 (online), 2631-780X (print)

Contents

Introduction: The United Nations, Natural Resources, and Human Mobility

For much of modern humanity's existence, the mobility of our populations was strongly linked to resource access, with migrations being often seasonal and exploratory for hunters and gatherers. While such nomadic lifestyles are now increasingly rare (or unfeasible), they have been the hallmark of many indigenous cultures worldwide. In a more modern context, the unprecedented scale and speed of global environmental changes linked to human-induced factors that are and will affect ecological ranges, land surface cover and condition, levels of aridity and desertification, and predictability and extremity of weather patterns are almost certainly going to have strengthening impacts on human mobility and distribution. The connection between resources and migration, then, fits within a wider question of how environmental change relates to human movement and mechanisms by which such a nexus can be governed.

Figure 1 gives an indication of the scale and scope of the complexity of the migration–mobility nexus as envisaged by the United Nations' International Organization for Migration (IOM). We will use the terms 'migration', 'movement', and 'mobility' interchangeably throughout this Element. This is to convey the movement of people for a variety of reasons over a range of temporal and spatial scales with a variety of outcomes and impacts. Our varied use of terms is deliberate. Some scholars state a preference for the use of the term 'mobility' over 'migration', suggesting that the latter term has too often been used to carry unfairly negative political connotations and also semantically fails to capture the full fluidity of human movement. The stance we take is that, while we wish to be reflective of terminology in the contemporary literature and research on the topic, we should also not allow ourselves to be held hostage to the weaponization of perfectly serviceable terminology.

In line with gloomy proclamations that have often accompanied discussions of migration in popular discourse and media, 'environmental migration' and 'environmental migrants'[1] have both been portrayed as a failure to adapt to environmental stress. The environmental governance arena has often seen migrants as 'symptoms' of detrimental global change processes (e.g. particularly around sea-level rise due to global warming). In this analysis, we seek to add to the questioning of the dominant policy orthodoxy of pathologizing human mobility as a manifestation of a stressed environment akin to a disease

---

[1] 'Persons or groups of persons who, predominantly for reasons of sudden or progressive change in the environment that adversely affects their lives or living conditions, are obliged to leave their habitual homes, or choose to do so, either temporarily or permanently, and who move either within their country or abroad' (IOM, 2019: 64).

Different types of migration

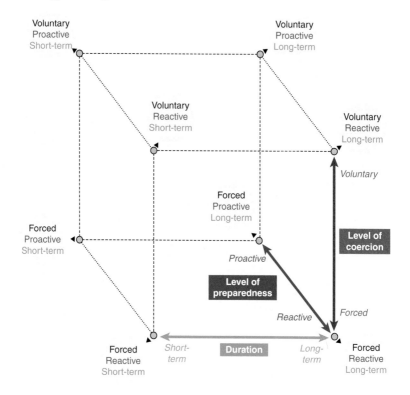

Figure 1 Different types of migration.
Source: Ionesco et al. (2017).

of the body. Instead, we seek to exemplify mobility in the Anthropocene as an integral element of a wider, more nuanced, complex adaptive (socio-ecological) system which by definition is dynamic and emergent in nature and, in turn, requires equivalent policy structures.

An Earth Systems Governance (ESG) approach conceptually lends itself to such holistic understandings of mobility. By Earth Systems Governance, we follow the established definition of 'the interrelated and increasingly integrated system of formal and informal rules, rule-making systems, and actor-networks at all levels of human society (from local to global) that are set up to steer societies towards preventing, mitigating, and adapting to global and local environmental change and, in particular, earth system transformation, within the normative context of sustainable development' (Biermann et al., 2010). This Element provides a preliminary exploration of how the nascent discourse on developing international mechanisms to manage migration such as the Global Compact for Migration might be operationalized within the framework of ESG.

Such a paradigm is intuitively appropriate for dealing with migration, which we see as an example of a complex adaptive response to a series of nested systems in which humans interact with the environment. We deliberately use the plural 'systems' rather than 'system' to indicate this nested nature of our analytical frames.

Underlying empirical evidence surrounding mobility within changing environmental conditions around the world also supports an Earth Systems Governance approach to looking at resource influences on migration. There is a strong consensus that migration and displacement are multi-causal. Adding to this complexity, natural resource availability and use, populations' livelihood dependence, and resource management are often intermediaries in the environment–migration nexus, if not always the primary ones (Ionesco et al., 2017). This is the case at points of origin for movement, but also in transit and at destinations. The role of resources in triggering a spectrum of human mobility – either by necessity, opportunity, or a combination thereof – has an important bearing on the forms of migration and displacement that result, and subsequently, the impacts of those movements (Brown & McLeman, 2013). This is not a teleological process in which mobility or displacement 'ends' upon arrival that the overwhelming emphasis on drivers of migration might imply. Rather, the impacts of mobility feed back into socio-ecological systems and affect resources of migrants, communities of origin, and destination communities (Guadagno, 2017). This underscores the need to investigate resource use, change, and management within socio-ecological systems at macro-, meso-, and micro-levels, and the role of human mobility within them, including its impact on the system in a web of causalities and feedbacks.

Within our ESG framing, we aim to introduce and examine the validity of using natural resources as a key intervening variable through which to understand, analyze, and govern local-to-global-scale relationships between environmental changes and movement of people. A focus on natural resources aims to add a conceptual and methodological shift in prevailing approaches: to date, the connections between environmental change and mobility have been typically dealt with on a 'high level', with climatic trends and projections being regressed onto regional population/demographic dynamics. Natural resources could act as an intuitive and more empirically grounded way of both exploring the linkages between the two aspects and placing them appropriately and contextually within wider earth systems debates. Yet literature and research specifically exploring resources against mobility is currently limited, as is our ability to accurately capture resource dynamics in the very places that observers cite as being most vulnerable to resource pressures in the coming century. Methodologically, including natural resource variables in regression analyses can be problematic because of the possible circularity of the relationship of the variables (e.g. migration being both a symptom and cause of resource depletion). In this context, this Element serves in three equal parts: firstly, a foundation for seeing resources as an appropriate framing of environmental changes as they manifest themselves 'on the ground' and their relationship to other sociological factors influencing mobility; secondly, an exploratory examination of where 'blind spots' currently exist in terms of our ability to understand these connections; and, thirdly, what our current and potential future options might be for better governing the nexus between resources and mobility. Importantly, the inclusion of natural resources and their management helps move the environment–migration policy conversation from being focused on climate change mitigation and adaptation to include local, national, and international governance of natural resources.

1 The Resource–Mobility–Governance Nexus

The Growth of Writing on 'Environmental Migration'

Our past experiences of and future projections for human-induced environmental change and sudden disaster events have undoubted implications for resource management and, in turn, human mobility. The governance nexus *between* these temporal scales in terms of resources and mobility has, however, been largely neglected in academic and policymaking arenas. In this opening section we present concise highlights of relevant literature since the turn of the millennium in order to highlight what could (and should) constitute the key features of this nexus.

An initial key aspect in discussing connections between environmental pressures and migration is to avoid a polemic and/or linear mindset. While a gradual or rapid debasement of environmental conditions is often depicted as a driver that ultimately leads to social instability and forced displacement, the two parameters are by no means related in a linear fashion. For example, this context can also spur the development of capacity for *more* sustainable resource management. Indeed, mobility is already considered by many as a form of adaptation to the impacts of climate change (Foresight, 2011; Ionesco et al., 2017; Renaud et al., 2011; Salerno et al., 2017). Unfortunately, major public-facing policy platforms such as the Global Centre on Adaptation have largely presented migration as a symptom of crisis rather than an adaptive strategy that could be leveraged for more effective resource management and ecological efficiency. Popular coverage and traditional policymaking surrounding international human mobility have also been and are, broadly speaking, based on a relatively binary understanding of why people move: they are either forced to move as a result of conflict or political persecution – and seen as 'refugees' or enticed to move by the promise of better living conditions elsewhere – and labelled as 'migrants' (Ionesco et al., 2017). The reality, of course, is more nuanced and complicated. Human mobility has existed throughout history, with people moving for, or being displaced by, a diverse range of interconnected factors that have been well documented (Black et al., 2011; Van Praag & Timmerman, 2019).

Aligned with emerging concerns over the various socio-economic and environmental impacts of anthropogenic activity in other fields of study, the potential implications of resource access, economic opportunity, and environmental degradation on migration and displacement have been the subject of study for more than two decades (e.g. Döös, 1997). As we can gauge from the contents and citations of this Element, the literature has expanded dramatically in the last twenty years (see Piguet, 2021 for an informative review), particularly as research has begun to uncover the potential ramifications of climate change on population distribution (McLeman & Gemenne, 2018). Over this time period, scholars have developed different narratives to explain the causes, forms, and impacts of migration, which in turn have sometimes been employed as a means to propose or justify various policy interventions (Vlassopoulos, 2013). There have been increasingly interdisciplinary attempts to reassess the framework of migration research and bring in new perspectives from social and cultural geography (Felgentreff & Pott, 2016). Piguet (2010), for example, identifies six distinct 'families' of research methods that have endeavoured to understand 'environmental migration': ecological inference based on area characteristics, individual sample surveys, time series analysis, multilevel analysis, agent-based modelling (ABM), and qualitative/ethnographic studies. This is along with the emergence of meta-studies of the existing literature to identify gaps in the empirical coverage (Cattaneo et al., 2019; Obokata et al., 2014; Piguet, 2021; Upadhyay et al., 2015). Yet much of this work remains diagnostic rather than prospective in terms of governance.

The Case for a Natural Resources Lens

Conceptual questions of when and how broader environmental change contributes to migration, displacement, or relocation are, then, now relatively established. Increasingly, so are observed instances: reports like the *Atlas of Environmental Migration* (Ionesco et al., 2017) and *Groundswell* (Rigaud et al., 2018) show a varied picture of migration outcomes within the wider context of environmental change. Yet specific focus on types, stocks and flows of resources, and their availability and management, that could provide potentially pivotal factors in mediating such linkages between environmental change and human mobility, have been given scant attention. This is somewhat surprising: when one talks of potential causal (rather than proximate) connecting forces between movement of people and climatic or environment changes, we are, intrinsically, referring to the available resource base. That is to say, it is not prevailing conditions or anomalies in temperature and rainfall that might directly account for movement of people: it is the impact that temperature and rainfall have on interconnected resource systems like agricultural land, water availability, and biomass for fuel and food. A connecting lens of resources works in precisely the same sense that it is the outcome of human overexploitation of natural materials that has resulted in altered prevailing climatic conditions in the first instance.

There are certainly strong indications within existing literature to support a closer and more specific look at the role of resources (and their degradation and unsustainable management) in affecting migration and displacement. A sizable portion of the associated literature since the turn of the millennium has, albeit often obliquely, referred to the diminishment of natural resource systems and connections with mobility. This has been through a focus on the role of localized environmental degradation, and particularly the overshadowing impacts of climate change, and their subsequent role in stimulating movement of varying kinds, from forced displacement through to planned relocation.

Existing commentary and studies on the connections between environment and migration are often (imperfectly) categorized by their temporal scope (Cattaneo et al., 2019). On the one side are the 'slow-onset' factors – drought, desertification, sea-level rise, land degradation, and growing water insecurity – that disrupt livelihoods. This is especially prevalent for resource-dependent occupations such as farming, livestock herding, and fishing. Sometimes the process is more immediately evident as being anthropogenic in cause: man-made infrastructure that impacts the environment, such as dams, might also lead to a decline in availability of land and water resources, impacting livelihoods and influencing the impetus to move. On the other side are 'sudden-onset' events – flooding, industrial accidents, storms and glacial lake outburst floods – that present more imminent dangers to people's lives and livelihoods, as well as disruption or destruction to resource and ecosystem services (Brown, 2008). These two types of events can potentially occur in parallel and influence one another, something which has spurred the development of multi-risk scenarios that attempt to capture their convergence (Rigaud et al., 2018).

'Slow-onset' erosion of livelihoods in origin locations has been one of the main drivers of migration that has been highlighted. This is often juxtaposed by the pull of relatively (or perceived) better and more secure livelihood opportunities in destination locations on the other. The reasons for a decline in livelihoods in origin locations are sometimes linked to natural resource degradation: for example, due to the loss of land by riverbank erosion or a lack of investment in soil fertility (Ahmed et al., 2019; Ayeb-Karlsson et al., 2016). Similarly, some quantitative studies have drawn a direct link between the impact of slow-onset environmental change on resources and the overall size of mobility flows. In each mentioned case, it is pertinent to note the connection of mobility to the resource base available for tenable agricultural livelihoods on which many people around the globe are still highly dependent. Feng and Oppenheimer (2010) analyzed the link between crop yields and cross-border Mexico–US migration and estimated that a 10 per cent drop in crop yields would lead to an additional 2 per cent of the population emigrating. A 2015 multilevel event history study of international migration from Mexico between 1986 and 1999 found that warming temperatures and excessive precipitation significantly increased international migration (Nawrotzki et al., 2016). In the Philippines, a rise in temperature and increased typhoon activity appears to be linked to increased out-migration (principally through the mechanism of reduced rice crop yields), though changes in rainfall did not appear to have a consistently significant effect on migration patterns (Ayeb-Karlsson et al., 2022; Bohra-Mishra et al., 2017). Cai et al. (2016) found a statistically significant relationship between temperature and international migration, but only in the most agriculturally dependent countries given the link between rising temperatures and diminishing agricultural yields. A village-level study of the Kilimanjaro district in Tanzania noted a positive relationship between rainfall shortage and out-migration, even after controlling for other important socio-economic variables. The study argues that food insecurity for humans and livestock is the mechanism through which rainfall variability affects human mobility (Afifi et al., 2014). In that vein, household surveys taken in the northern Central American countries of Guatemala, El Salvador, and Honduras identified a notable increase in out-migration following the onset of drought, its impact on agricultural land, and subsequent food security (IOM & WFP, 2022).

The literature also describes a number of resource disparities that may encourage people to move in the hope of expanded or more reliable livelihood options in more 'resource rich' destination areas. For example, several case studies have looked at the role of mineral resources (particularly informal, artisanal mining) in shaping internal and cross-border migration. In Russia, a study of mining sites across seventy-eight regions between 2004 and 2010 detailed net internal migration rising in mining areas (Sardadvar & Vakulenko, 2017). Nyame et al. (2009) looked at how the different stages of mine development (growth, stagnation, and closure) in Ghana led to their own characteristic migration patterns. These, they argue, are contributing to the country becoming a transit area for prospective migrant miners in addition to its traditional role of being a destination country for miners. Likewise, large numbers of men migrated from Lesotho to South Africa during the twentieth century to work in the commercial mines, sending remittances back to Lesotho. Since many of these large mines have closed, these men have tended to move across to the informal sector, mining abandoned mines around Johannesburg (Makhetha, 2020). Meanwhile, a detailed survey of nearly a thousand male and female artisanal miners in the eastern part of the Democratic Republic of Congo found that artisanal mining sites were the destination for internal migrants, but that escape from economic hardship was a more significant factor than the perceived potential economic gains (Maclin et al., 2017). Other work has assessed the opportunity of differing resource ownership or management systems (i.e. ability to own land elsewhere, availability of services and resources offered in urban settings, etc.) as being a factor in encouraging resource-related migration. The Mecúfi district of northern Mozambique has seen a significant migration of people to coastal areas since the civil war, in part to access coastal and marine resources (Bryceson & Massinga, 2002).

Very importantly, however, resource-movement linkages that can be teased from the studies also frequently highlight that they are complex and not always consistent. Upadhyay et al. (2015) note that a lot of the literature tends to downplay ambiguities in the terminology and overestimates what is often limited empirical evidence. For example, a study of soil quality in Kenya and Uganda appeared to show that high soil quality reduced migration in Kenya but increased migration in neighbouring Uganda (Gray, 2011). Gray and Wise (2016) used detailed household information to revisit the links between climate change and internal and international migration over a six-year period in five African countries: Kenya, Uganda, Nigeria, Burkina Faso, and Senegal. Their results were mixed: temperature anomalies tended to increase migration in Uganda but decrease migration in Kenya and Burkina Faso. But they showed no consistent relationship in Senegal or Nigeria. Precipitation, meanwhile, showed a very weak and inconsistent relationship with migration across all the case study countries.

There have also been attempts to investigate the impact on human mobility of 'sudden-onset' events such as floods, hurricanes, and disaster-induced industrial accidents (Black et al., 2013; Zhang et al., 2014) that have inevitable and immediate impacts on a given area's resource base. However, the links to natural resources tend to be overlooked or more implicit. In Vietnam, regular flood events were linked to displacement, individual migration decisions, and government-initiated resettlement of households (Dun, 2011). In this case, the resettlement initiatives moved people only short distances in order to maintain social cohesion and access to agricultural land to decrease poverty (Zickgraf, 2019). A review of select Asian countries for a period between 2005 and 2017 noted that natural hazards such as storms and floods generally increased external migration. The study argued for a direct link to natural resources, noting that 'natural resource depletion increases external migration' (Abbas Khan et al., 2019).

Another notable aspect in reviewing existing information that what could well be classed as resource-related mobility is often labelled *economic* migration, with its environmental roots frequently masked by their entanglement with other issues: the economic impacts of resource use and management in the community of origin, economic opportunities presented in destinations or the legal definitions of the migrants themselves. Afifi (2011) identified a number of internal and cross-border mobility trends in Niger, explicitly including natural resource considerations relating to water (droughts, the shrinking of Lake Chad, problems in the Niger River) and land (soil degradation, deforestation, and sand intrusion). However, the study argued that economic factors are the mechanism through which environmental factors encourage migration, suggesting that the appropriate term for such migration should be 'environmentally induced economic migration' (Afifi, 2011). This is to suggest that differentiating between economic and environmental migration, therefore, has little value in countries whose economics are resource dependent: in agriculture-based economies, environmental migration *is* economic migration.

Climate change is, of course, just one of many factors influencing mobility decisions (Kniveton et al., 2008). Resource use and management can affect mobility responses within and outside of climate contexts. Resource depletion through overuse (Bilsborrow & DeLargy, 1990), or resource loss as a result of infrastructure projects, conservation measures and land grabbing have also been identified as important in stimulating migration and displacement (Salerno et al. 2014). Hamilton and colleagues (2004) cite the example of the Faroe Islands. An affluent society that is highly dependent on fisheries, the islands experienced a crisis in the 1990s when their fisheries became depleted through a combination of overfishing and environmental stress. The result was unemployment, business failures and out-migration, particularly of young adults, which permanently changed the make-up of the islands' population. Vigil (2018), meanwhile, provides an analysis into the controversial phenomenon of large-scale land acquisition (described as 'green grabbing') in numerous locations by overseas investors, particularly for biofuels and forest carbon projects that, in some cases, have displaced local groups living or working on that land (e.g. Nyantakyi-Frimpong & Kerr, 2017).

Linkages between livelihoods, mobility, and 'climate stress' have also been expanded to consider the potential for conflict in the context of 'environmental migration'. The Intergovernmental Panel on Climate Change has attempted to synthesize these issues conceptually in their fifth assessment report in 2014, as shown in Figure 2.

In fact, Baldwin et al. (2014) argue that the 'spectre' of migration framed in such negative ways is playing a crucial role in the securitization of climate change, with climate-induced migration being used as a sort of shorthand to describe the security impacts of a warming climate. Much of the negative framing and fear-based portrayals of human mobility indeed surrounds its potential (adverse) impact on peace and (international) security. In particular, migration and displacement are commonly cited as mediating factors in a pathway towards conflict (Adger et al., 2014). Certainly, there are examples of population movements leading to tensions and conflicts over more scarce resources, often linked to competing livelihoods and/or ethnic groups with histories of tension. For example, Mbonile (2005) noted how people moving to the Pangani River Basin in Tanzania, partially in search of water, led to intensive conflicts between pastoralists and farmers, increasing demand for water, and negatively affecting water availability in downstream areas.

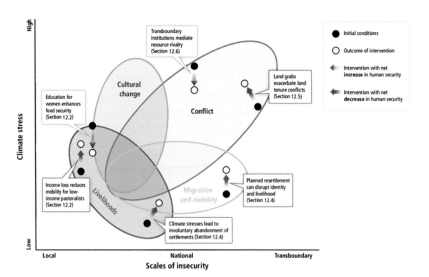

Figure 2 The conceptual space for migration and mobility as considered by the Intergovernmental Panel on Climate Change with reference to sections in their *Fifth Assessment Report.*
Source: Pachauri et al. (2015), Technical summary (p73).

McLeman et al. (2016) similarly note that resource-related mobility can be linked to political instability but caution against overly simplistic cause–effect assumptions. Going further, Dalby (2002) argues that deterministic claims about the relationship between environmental change, instability, and migration are, in fact, implausible given that conflict and mobility are complex, socio-ecological, and innately political phenomena. In fact, Nicholson (2014) warns that any ongoing substantive search for a causal relationship could be a 'blind alley' that fails to analyze its assumptions and, in so doing, allows the results to be politically manipulated. Therefore, links between natural resource availability, conflict, security, and human mobility must be analyzed cautiously rather than assumed as such.

Given the aforementioned discussion, it can be safely asserted that there is no universal linear relationship between climatic influences, natural resources, and human mobility. However, various studies have credibly identified mechanisms through which resource dependence and vulnerability to slow-onset environmental change influence the likelihood of more voluntary forms of migration. Reliance on natural resources can contribute to increasing a community, or household or individual's vulnerability, but acts in concert with other features. For example, Gemenne et al. (2017) argued that vulnerability and the probability of migration of individuals in West Africa are influenced by the extent of their dependence on natural resources, their socio-economic status, and their demographic characteristics. In fact, much of the literature on human mobility in response to slow-onset changes cites the importance of natural resource-dependent livelihoods in explaining populations' (rural but also urban) vulnerability, demonstrating the links between climate change, economic and environmental drivers of mobility.

Changes in the quality, availability, and access of resources do seem, therefore, to have the capacity to exacerbate pre-existing vulnerabilities and inequalities. Mobility linked to resources can, therefore, be seen within, and explained as a product of, a larger framework of vulnerability. A society's vulnerability determines how badly it is affected by environmental hazards. Vulnerability is described as the state of susceptibility to harm from exposure to stresses associated with environmental change and from the lack of capacity to adapt to those stresses (Adger, 2006). The UK government's *Foresight* report on Migration and Global Environmental Change (2011) was one of the first (of now several) sources to suggest that populations may, in fact, become 'trapped' when vulnerability is greater than people's ability to move (Figure 3).

In this vulnerability framework, 'climate stress' (Figure 3) is determined by a complex mixture of environmental, social, political, and economic forces and an individual's level of 'capital' within the context of each force. The observed impacts and severity of changes in resource dynamics depend on interrelated socio-environmental systems and responses to human movement (or immobility)

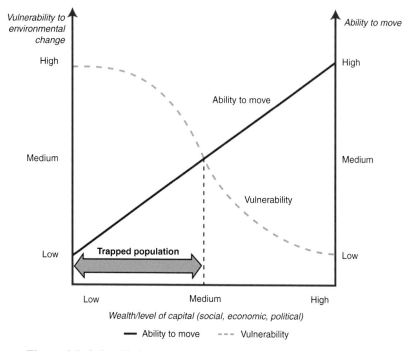

Figure 3 Relationship between well-being and vulnerability in 'trapping' populations.

Source: Foresight (2011).

(Cardona et al., 2012; Rahman & Hickey, 2020). These stressors, in turn, strongly influence the ability of different populations to weather, adapt, or 'transform' in response to the degradation of and reduction in available resources of various kinds (United Nations, 2016).

Visualizing a Resource–Mobility–Governance Nexus

The heterogeneous connections that environmental influences or 'climate stressors' have on livelihoods, conflict, and vulnerability have been highlighted not only to indicate important findings in the literature. They also heavily point to the fact that, in attempting to conceptually and empirically establish resources as a linking aspect between climatic/environmental change and human mobility, it is evident that we will need to consider multiple pathways, intermediate stages, engagement points, and resultant outcomes (Figure 4). The confluence between these factors can, then, be conceptually thought of as sharing the properties of a complex evolving socio-ecological system (Giampietro, 2019; Preiser et al., 2018) operating at different temporal, spatial, and social scales. This system will possess nested hierarchies; involve multi-directional

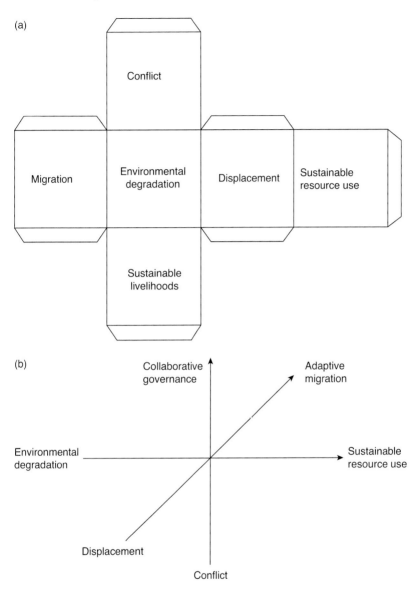

Figure 4 Resource–migration nexus on a 'governance dice' (a) and themes (b).

feedbacks, multilevel interactions, and inevitable uncertainty; and display properties of emergent non-equilibrium systems (Berkes et al., 2002; Gunderson & Holling, 2002; Kniveton et al., 2012; Mayumi & Giampietro, 2006; Rammel et al., 2007) in which governance approaches will need to situate themselves within and respond to.

Advocating for resources to be placed at the centre of 'environmental migration' debates aligns itself with evolving Earth Systems Governance frameworks (as outlined by Burch et al., 2019) in several ways. The implications of unsustainable resource use are longstanding yet accelerating in the Anthropocene era. The issue of significantly increased environmentally induced migration as a potential outcome of resource use is certainly an emerging concern. It is undeniably complex and highly contextual in its dynamics and drivers, being embedded in interconnected social, political, economic, technological, and environmental systems. As such, it is a potential phenomenon that will require interdisciplinary observation and governance on multiple levels. And, as with similarly emerging socio-ecological and climate-related fields of study, it currently resides in the stage of conceptual discussion within policymaking arenas when there is a pressing need for more concrete frameworks and actions.

In terms of governance approaches, a number of relevant questions arise when looking at the resource–mobility nexus. For example, what are the policy contexts and conditions whereby better management of (local, regional, global) natural resources have or could play a role in avoiding forced displacement? Given that mobility occurs for myriad reasons, how might we safeguard against further unsustainable resource use in identified likely locations of immigration?

Underlying much of the debate over the impacts of mobility has been a calculation, often unspoken, as to whether the cumulative impacts of migration and displacement represent a net positive (to be encouraged) or a net negative (to be discouraged). De Haas (2010) notes that the debate on migration and impacts on development have swung back and forth between 'development optimistic' approaches in 1950s and 1960s, to 'neo-Marxist pessimism' in the 1970s and 1980s and back towards a more optimistic outlook since then. These differing perspectives are present in the literature: Nicholson, (2014) notes that the discussion about resources and migration is often framed by a concern about its causal impacts on the societal status quo. Nishimura, (2015) argues that the primary focus should shift from being the 'national security' of developed countries to the particular needs of migrant populations themselves which would help migration to be included in adaptation strategies. The specific drivers and forms of displacement and migration determine the balance of these impacts on resources and, through those, sustainable development, politics, security, for instance.

The important starting point in these discussions is to not demonize migrants who are universally recognized as adding to the social, economic, and cultural fabric of societies. Resource management systems might 'hold the key' to drawing some of the political poison out of contested views of migration and displacement and maximizing its benefits. However, appropriate policy responses require these relationships to be better understood. We still do not really understand how different resource-related policies and programme initiatives influence the potential for migration and displacement, and what best practices we should profile and mainstream (McLeman et al., 2016). Part of the governance challenge in dealing with environmentally induced migration is that it suffers from significant fragmentation of actors both vertically (between local, national, and international levels) and horizontally (rarely dealt with as a single issue but rather addressed by multiple initiatives in different ways) (McAdam, 2009). Gemenne et al. (2017) note that building structures to welcome and putting in place mechanisms for migrants and internally displaced persons (IDPs) are necessary steps to attenuate future risks. They argued that regional authorities have to work together to reinforce the resilience of societies of origin as well as facilitating migration as a form of adaptation. Ultimately policymakers need to address both sides of the environment–migration nexus: on the one hand, where possible, to implement adaptation strategies that allow people to remain where they currently are and on the other, to identify migration and relocation strategies that protect people's livelihoods and lives in those places they are unable to stay.

2 Preventative Measures against Forced Displacement and Their Governance

We have established that resource scarcity and security of access to natural capital have been a major concern in driving migration. How might we modulate processes of globalized appropriation of natural capital such as large-scale land acquisitions to prevent forced migration? What might be mechanisms of earth systems governance with projects such as hydroelectric dams or major mining projects? Ensuring local rights, ownership, and tenure over these resources has the capacity to create a much greater vested interest in protecting the resource base. Alternatively, but a process that can also work in tandem with those above, fostering livelihoods that are less reliant upon resources can alleviate pressure on resource stocks. External inputs to and assistance within the associated socio-environmental system, such as remittances and targeted development assistance, may also be of pragmatic utility in alleviating resource pressures. In the case of natural hazards, more rapid assistance may be needed to help populations move to escape floods, storms, and cyclones.

There are also certain vulnerable populations who may feel the immediate (in terms of disasters) or mounting (in terms of slow-onset changes) need and desire to move but do not have the capacity to do so due to a range of reasons. These groups (referring back to Figure 3) are sometimes referred to as 'trapped' in reference to their inability to escape undesirable or hazardous circumstances (Ayeb-Karlsson et al., 2018; Black et al., 2013; Foresight, 2011). In both instances, strengthening the vitality and sustainability of the resource base, through approaches such as conservation and reclamation techniques, have the potential to stimulate improvements in socio-economic resilience, especially in areas with livelihoods that are strongly tied to natural resources (such as agriculture, fisheries).

Soil and Water Resource Conservation, and Reclamation, Policies

Protection and, where degraded, reclamation of soil and water resources are likely to have a connection to reducing forced displacement in a handful of ways. Maintaining stability of soil and biomass, particularly in coastal and mountainous regions, protects against extreme weather and connected natural hazards like flooding and landslides that often result in notable movement of people in the most severe contexts. On a less extreme level and over longer temporal scales, sustainability of soil and water resources ensure the ongoing viability of numerous vital ecosystem services. This of course includes broader biodiversity, which is increasingly being understood as an element worthy of protection both on an intrinsic and instrumental level, and loss of land mass to erosion. Soil and water are also, of course, intrinsically connected: soils requiring appropriate levels of moisture to maintain their fertility and stability: unstable soils are most at risk of water erosion: and lack of water and unsustainable land practices can result in degradation, erosion and desertification (Gruver, 2013).

Substantial efforts such as Africa's 'Great Green Wall', the inaugural project of the UN's Decade on Ecosystem Restoration, which aims to restore some 8,000 km of degraded land across the continent's Sahelian regions, or the ambition to raise US$50 billion to restore drought-stricken areas around Lake Chad represent eye-catching illustrations of responses to pervasive degradation of soil and water resources. But particularly vital to consider in terms of soil and water resources is, of course, agricultural practices which account for half of the cover of Earth's productive land, consume 70 per cent of global freshwater withdrawals, and engage a huge number of livelihoods, particularly in poorer and environmentally vulnerable contexts (FAO, 2017b). Diminishment of these important resource stocks can act to increase poverty and encourage movement of populations where livelihoods are unable to remediate or adapt to these gradual changes (Barrett & Bevis, 2015).

The impetus and many ideas behind conservation and reclamation of soil and water resources are by no means new, nor restricted to places one might intuitively see as 'marginal' environs.[2] Despite a long history of research indicating its (environmental and socio-economic) appropriateness and advocacy for greater

---

[2] The example of the Dust Bowl in America's agricultural heartlands, for example.

implementation (e.g. Scherr & Yadav, 1996), prevailing practices in both larger scale, commercial and subsistence agriculture have typically been quite negligent in conserving quality and quantity of soil and water resources (Albaladejo et al., 2021; Borrelli et al., 2017, 2020).

In their review of 'global achievements' in soil and water conservation practices, Kassam et al. (2014) summarize the three key interlinked principles of 'Conservation Agriculture' as: (i) minimizing or avoiding mechanical soil disturbance; (ii) maintaining continuous soil cover of organic top layers with plants; and (iii) adopting practices that include a diversity of (appropriately context-selected) plant species and farming systems that can contribute to enhancing soil quality and 'system resilience' that is invariably connected to soil health. The authors suggest that when conducted appropriately, benefits of conservation agriculture can include increased factor productivities and yields, decreases in fuel energy or manual labour up to 70 per cent, up to 50 per cent less fertilizer use, 20 per cent or more reduction in pesticide and herbicide use, 30 per cent less water requirements, and reduced cost outlay on farm machinery. As importantly, such practices can enhance climate change adaptability because of improved soil-plant moisture relations, greater carbon sequestration and lower GHG emissions, and decreasing flood risks and improved water resources (Kassam et al., 2014). In line with this, Abdul-Rahim et al.'s (2018) assessment of farm outputs and poverty rates in parts of China where conservation of soil and water resources is more effectively implemented lead them to suggest that such practices 'can contribute to the agricultural economic growth and rural poverty reduction' and that they, along with capital inputs, 'are now more important in poverty reduction and economic growth than farmland area and agricultural labour'.

On an international and national policymaking level, 'conservation' and 'sustainable' agriculture approaches adopted by the likes of the FAO (2017a), OECD (2010) and UNCCD (2014), amongst others, have increasingly taken an explicitly more holistic systems approach that aims to enhance productivity, maintain ecosystem services, and strengthen farmers' resilience to environmental changes. Yet, as Table 1 shows (official), adoption of practices that are likely to contribute to the sustainability of soil and water resources within the especially relevant agricultural sector are rare, with notable areas like Asia and Africa being particularly low.

Albaladejo et al. (2021), the FAO (2017a&b), Kassam et al. (2014), and Keesstra et al. (2016), all provide excellent analyses of the potential and pitfalls of pragmatic and policymaking approaches towards soil and water resources in agriculture: a lack of baseline and available information on resource stocks and quality; consequent challenges with our ability to model, monitor, and manage them; inappropriateness and/or ineffectiveness of international-to-local-scale

Table 1 Global area distribution of CA by continent

Continent	Area (ha)	Percentage of total	CA as percentage of arable cropland
South America	55,464,100	45	57.3
North America	39,981,000	32	15.4
Australia and NZ	17,162,000	14	69.0
Russia and Ukraine	5,100,000	4	3.3
Asia	4,723,000	4	0.9
Europe	1,351,900	1	0.5
Africa	1,012,840	1	0.3
World	124,794,840	100	8.8

Source: Kassam et al. (2014)

legislative approaches towards soil and water resources; and a sense of justified or perceived livelihood insecurity resulting from lack of local ownership over such resources and assistance in their management.

The untenability of prevailing global agricultural practices and production in terms of land-use change; shifting consumption patterns; accountable carbon, methane, and other GHG emissions; and levels of artificial inputs and land degradation is a picture that is becoming increasingly empirically clear. Understandably, as most accountable consumers within global agricultural production systems, the predominant focus for remediating these trends has been on middle- and higher-income States. Yet the most affected in terms of short- to medium-term impacts of unsustainable agricultural practices are going to be our planet's most vulnerable people and environments. Failure to address the continuing, and potentially irreversible, debasement in ecosystems services and associated livelihoods and food security may well lead to displaced and/or trapped populations in many areas of the world where livelihoods are resource dependent. A huge improvement in the breadth and depth of empirical data, intervention, and funding is urgently required on a socio-economic and environmental basis.

Land Tenure Policies and Human Mobility

Historical experiences (like those of the US Dust Bowl) suggest that some of the most acute connections between natural resources and human mobility are related to land degradation and restoration practices. Yet there are also significant concerns over land tenure in many regions of the globe. For populations to remain in a region, ownership of land creates a vested interest for attachment and even where there is seasonal or cyclical mobility, a cause for return. Policies around land tenure can be instrumental in how populations interact with the natural resource base and consequently also in managing human mobility. But these relationships are complex and often appear to be acting in multiple directions: lack of access to land tenure can both spur migration as well as lead to trapped populations, depending on the context of the destination opportunities.

Recent reviews of the significant associated literature (e.g. Higgins et al., 2018; Simbizi et al., 2014; Tseng et al., 2020) indicate that, though the net positivity of outcomes is highly dependent upon localized context and effectiveness of policymaking, improving control over land resources by a wider swath of the population has predominantly positive effects on socio-economic and environmental parameters. This is particularly the case for regions such as sub-Saharan Africa, where both persistent, outdated tenure arrangements (including 'Green Grabbing', discussed in the section titled 'Policies to Mitigate "Green Grabbing"') and land degradation have been causes for concern, and East Asia, which has experienced rapid industrialization and population dynamic changes. Policymakers need to be reflexive in their implementation of land tenure security arrangements, giving local populations control over to and providing vested interest into land-based livelihood resources appear to be a key strategy to prevent outwards migration linked to resource degradation or limited supply per capita.

For example, in a study of the massive urban migration trends in China, which is by numbers the largest human mobility pattern of the twentieth century, Mullan et al. (2011) found that rural property rights played an important role in migration decisions. By examining the relationship between tenure insecurity and restrictions on land rentals, and participation in outside labour markets, the authors found that tenure insecurity reduces rural–urban migration. This relationship is particularly pronounced on forestland, which has implications for the conservation of recently replanted forest areas. However, increasing formalization of land tenure systems can also promote migration: in a separate study, Ma et al. (2015) found that tenure security perceptions play a significant role only in those villages without operational land rental markets. They state that 'in villages with underdeveloped land rental markets, households that expect that no land reallocations will occur within their village in the near future are less involved in migration, while households that attach a greater importance to land certificates in protecting land-use rights are more involved in migration'.

The localized and sociological dynamics and migration implications of policies intended to promote ownership of resources need to be thoroughly vetted prior to and monitored after their implementation.

The case study of Kenya is also useful to illustrate some key aspects of legislation and policies which could address the land tenure nexus with migration, being a State that has high levels of internal displacement; large refugee populations (from neighbouring Somalia) and international migration. The motivation for the policy reforms here were manifold but IOM and various partner organizations used the country as well as an example in their flagship collaborative project on *Migration, Environment and Climates Change: Evidence for Policy* (MECLEP).

Kenya's land laws exemplify policies that may have influenced displacement and landlessness, as well as settlement in environmentally vulnerable areas. In 1999, the government made a concerted effort to address these policy failures through the establishment of a 'Committee on Land Clashes' and the Njonjo Commission of Inquiry into the Land Law System of Kenya. Four years later, there was an additional Commission of Inquiry into the Illegal/Irregular Allocation of Public Land. A national land policy formulation process started in 2004 and led to a comprehensive set of policy guidance proposals laid forth in Paper No. 3 of 2009 on National Land Policy. The gravity of this work is reflected in the fact that the Constitution of 2010 included a chapter on Land and Environment (Chap. V), and Article 60 of this chapter sets forth seven principles in this regard:

(a) Equitable access to land;
(b) Security of land rights;
(c) Sustainable and productive management of land resources;
(d) Transparent and cost-effective administration of lands;
(e) Sound conservation and protection of ecologically sensitive areas;
(f) Elimination of gender discrimination in law, customs and practices related to land and property;
(g) Encouragement of communities to settle land disputes through local community initiatives

Kenya has considered the linkage between land tenure and migration in formulating policy given the complex history of internal mobility of its many tribal groups. In 2012, the country's parliament passed the Act on the Prevention, Protection and Assistance to Internally Displaced Persons and Affected Communities. However, policy analysis conducted by the IOM suggests several shortcomings of this Act (Schade, 2016). Firstly, the IDP Act does not elaborate on compensation, nor does it refer to the Land Act sec. 155(4) for such matters. Secondly, and conversely, the Land Act does not provide detail on guidelines for planned relocation or forced resettlement, but is more focused on formalizing and upgrading existing settlements and vacating public land required for public purposes on the other. Thirdly, detailed and comprehensive procedures for eviction and relocation in line with the Evictions and Resettlements Procedures Bill are still missing.

In 2016, Kenya promulgated the Community Land Act (CLA) legislation that allows local communities to register and take the title to their communal lands. More than 3.5 million people would now be eligible to have title to their communal lands, covering roughly 150,000 square miles, or 67 per cent of Kenya's landmass. These types of policies have the potential to create more economic resilience for pastoral groups that are otherwise more vulnerable to resource-linked displacements. The CLA defines 'community' as meaning 'a consciously distinct or organized group of users who share any of the following attributes: common ancestry, similar culture or unique mode of livelihood, socio-economic or other similar common interest, geographical space, ecological space or ethnicity' (CLA s. 2).[3] Community of interest is defined as 'the possession or enjoyment of common rights, privileges or interests in land, living in the same geographical area or having such apparent association' (CLA s. 2). This is a comprehensive definition which recognizes ecological factors and human mobilities within communal lands. Overall, the law has potential for enabling appropriate policies for implementation. However, ultimately, the government has to undertake a process of relinquishment of its current control over communal lands and the law proposes a transitional period of trusteeship. This is where ambiguities could delay effective policy implementation. Wily (2018) in a detailed review of the law and potential policies notes that those lands with extensive natural resources such as timber will be particularly challenging in this regard:

> Forests on community lands promise to be first in the firing line, given the well-known reluctance of forest authorities to use its constitutional right to transfer lands from public to private and community categories of ownership, and despite a global conservation environment in which community owner-conservator norms are recognized as a viable, cheap and sustainable route to forest rehabilitation and conservation for the long term.

Nevertheless, the Chinese and Kenyan cases of policy reforms towards land tenure have potential for decoupling the resource nexus with human mobility and making decisions on movement exogenous to particular natural resource constraints. Rwanda has also considered this approach as it is a post-conflict densely populated country with a history of land conflicts. Other governments,

---

[3] https://namati.org/wp-content/uploads/2020/03/Facilitator-Guide_Kenyan-Community-Land-Act.pdf.

particularly with indigenous communal lands, can learn from this experience and create greater resilience within their populations.

Policies to Mitigate 'Green Grabbing'

There has been ongoing concern that, without financial support and localized security over resources, many communities in immigration source countries can be targets of land grabs by large multinational agricultural interests. Some of these acquisitions may be for ostensibly environmental projects as well such as biofuel production, solar farms, or even for carbon offsets. But the growth of such 'green grabbing' has led to a global movement from civil society to articulate principles for donors and governments to assist in preventative policies. A coalition of 150 representatives of civil society, governments, and international policymaking organizations from more than forty-five countries met in Tirana, Albania, in 2011 and signed a declaration on *Securing land access for the poor in times of intensified natural resources competition.* This declaration recognized the migration nexus as well in this regard as follows:

> We note that land and other natural resources are increasingly scarce and under threat due to a number of factors, including population growth, migration, changes in consumption patterns, climate change, land degradation, corruption and other forms of poor governance. Moreover, this is taking place in a context in which the control of land is increasingly concentrated in the hands of a few, while at the same time, a growing number of rural and urban poor are left with small and fragmented lands. This fosters conflict and food insecurity and exacerbates poverty.

Policies that prevent such large-scale land acquisition require land-use planning regulations to be in sync with international investment laws which can often hold primacy at the level of federal law.

Related to these concerns of green grabbing, International Fund for Agricultural Development (IFAD) has also supported a US$20 million programme focused on improving existing farming practices in Rwanda, privileging livestock production for food – milk and meat – and manure to sustain organic farming in kitchen gardens and small plots. Similarly, IOM has supported agroecology policies that can raise the productivity of small-hold farmers and mitigate the chance that they would be economically crowded out by large land acquisitions resulting in migration.

Diversification of Livelihoods with Changing Resources

Economic diversification is widely recognized as a means of improving resilience in societies and creating multiple pathways for development when there are shocks to particular sectors. Indeed, seasonal and economic migration is often cited as one such diversification, albeit with the risk of increasing vulnerability to 'new' (from the migrant perspective) climate stresses, but with the added benefits of sectoral and geographic diversification (Banerjee et al., 2017). For example, people in Bangladesh and the Philippines have reported how they seasonally migrate to tend to urban or factory-based livelihoods during periods of dry spells or floods, as the environmental stress makes it difficult to sustain agricultural activities at this time (Ayeb-Karlsson et al., 2016, 2022). However, policies that promote economic diversification can also mitigate the need to migrate out of necessity. Diversification provides multiple career trajectories for youth and also allows for hybridity of income for families whose primary income sources may be seasonal or vulnerable to commodity price fluctuations (such as extractive industries) or security concerns (such as tourism). A study by Biswas and Mallick (2021) in Bangladesh revealed that diversification of income by shrimp farmers was an important mitigating factor in migration to urban areas in the country while at the same time damaging the ecosystem (Figure 5).

A key aspect of diversification policies is multiple skilling of the labour force and flexible wage payment options by employers. Women's education and having multiple income earners in a household can also help with diversification of income. Tax policies which encourage such multiple income households can also be important ways of ensuring greater income resilience and diversification.

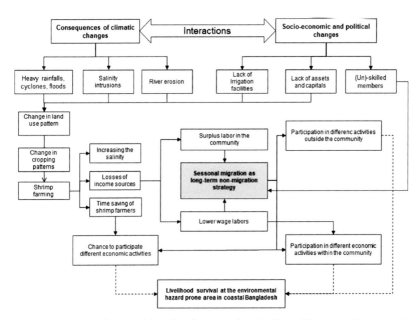

Figure 5 Nodes of potential policy intervention in diversification of income in coastal Bangladesh among shrimp farmers.
Source: Biswas and Mallick, 2021.

Remittance Bonds

In cases where there is either international mobility of population from developing to developed countries, or notable internal movement within countries, particularly from rural to urban areas, remittances can play an integral role in mitigating negative impacts on resource stocks in source countries. However, these policies will depend on the economic viability of migrants which can be highly sensitive to major economic shocks, such as the Covid-19 pandemic. According to World Bank estimates, 'remittance flows in 2020 to low- and middle-income countries fell by 7.2 per cent to US$508 billion, followed by a further decline of 7.5 per cent to US$470 billion in 2021'. Nevertheless, this is still a highly significant number and for some individual recipient countries, remittances can be (predicted to be) as high as a third of their GDP. Additionally, while there is still a dearth of qualitative data, limited studies on internal remittances suggest that, while they are typically smaller in value (30 per cent less than) than international remittances, they are five times as prevalent among households and much more likely to flow from urban to rural areas (Adams, 2007; IBRD & World Bank, 2006).

Policy formulation should consider the stocks of financial savings of the diaspora population as well as the demographics of the migrants in specific locations. Figure 6 shows some of the world's major countries with potential for implementing a variety of remittance funds management policies. However, if the global data are analyzed in terms of the contribution of remittances to the share of GDP of the country, 'the top 5 countries which received the highest remittances as a share of gross domestic product (GDP) in 2019 were Tonga (37.6% of GDP), Haiti (37.1%), South Sudan (34.1%), the Kyrgyz Republic (29.2%), and Tajikistan (28.2%)'.

The most well-used and studied remittance finance policy in the context of migration are bonds which can help to create a funding mechanism for ecological restoration and a variety of development activities in source countries linked to natural resources. These bonds are often termed 'diaspora bonds' as well and operate like traditional bonds with an aim of providing fairly predictable financing for governments in source countries. The bonds are bought by migrants with a return on investment that also helps their home country. In finance terms these bonds are 'untagged', meaning that the issuer has latitude around the use of funds. In order for the bonds to work, however, there is a modicum of trust in the home country's financial and political system that is needed for the migrants to take on the risk of purchasing such securities. The Brookings Institution undertook an analysis of such instruments in 2016 and noted the following key advantages of the remittance/diaspora bonds:

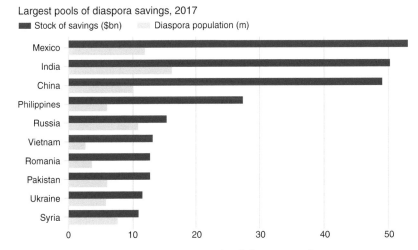

Figure 6 The largest pools of diaspora savings.
Source: Johnson (2019), based on World Bank data.

- Encourages external private investment in a developing country, via an intermediary institution (i.e. to structure the Social Impact Bond (SIB)/ Development Impact Bond (DIB) and manage risk)
- Allows the targeting of remittance funds beyond family networks and in support of a societal good attractive to the investor (e.g. health systems; education; early childhood development; employment)
- Uses a structured financing vehicle that provides known rates of return and known levels of principal recovery/risk
- Targets the diaspora, but could be presented as a retail investment option more generally (the Development Corporation for Israel's bond issues were targeted towards, but not limited to, the Jewish diaspora; India's bond issues were limited to investors of Indian origin)
- Accesses a multi-billion dollars global resource pool, in which everyone (potentially) wins: returns for the investor if the intervention succeeds; achievement of a societal and developmental good (the activities supported by the SIB/DIB), and potentially reduced risk for outcome funders (through 'payment for success').

The IFAD, which is a United Nations agency in close affiliation with the Food and Agricultural Organization (FAO), has piloted sixty projects on development usage of funds from remittances through its Financing Facility for Remittances. International Fund for Agricultural Development's projects typically have two prongs. As with remittance bonds these projects aim to capitalize on the potential investment capital of migrant workers. Funds that go into this mediated pool, which has the imprimatur and hence trust of the United Nations, can be used for development activities. For example, the *Financial Times* investigated a project in the Philippines which tapped funds from 1,260 recipient families and 1,500 migrant workers, mostly in Italy. When supplemented with grants from donors, the project funnelled US$8 million into works such as agricultural cooperatives, creating 1,300 jobs. In Somalia, US$1 million raised from the diaspora helped to finance the creation of fourteen companies and 230 jobs in fishing, agriculture, and food processing. The paper also noted that Nigeria's first diaspora bond was oversubscribed by 130 per cent and raised US$300 million, though Ethiopia had fewer convincing results with its 2008 and 2011 bonds.

These bonds work best if structured carefully and allow early withdrawal if investors want to back other projects in the country. The linkage between remittances and resources and migration was also considered in a think-piece previously published by the International Resource Panel. The flow diagram in Figure 7 shows how remittances can play both positive and negative roles in land degradation. The goal of policies should be to encourage the positive role through remittance bonds and to create incentives for more ecologically sustainable uses of private remittance funds that are received by families. The burden on migrants for propelling the economies of origin can also seem daunting and raises questions of social justice and domestic responsibility of governments. The concept of 'social remittances' whereby norms, ideas, technology, and skills also move between migrants and non-migrants (both positive and negative in the context of development) deserve attention (Levitt, 1998). Policies that promote key positive social remittance prospects, such as green entrepreneurship, should be encouraged. Existing domestic policies for more sustainable natural capital investments by citizens through tax and subsidy confluence can also be employed in this regard.

Targeted Development Assistance Policies and Migration

The role of development assistance in mitigating migration has been debated as an antidote to stringent border control policies. In an empirical study on a large sample of country pairs, comprised of 22 donors and more than 150 recipients, over the period 1993–2008, Bermeo and Leblang (2015) find that donors do indeed use foreign aid as a way of attempting to achieve broader immigration goals, targeting areas of outward migration to try and boost development and decrease the demand for entry into the donor country. Their study found a 'statistically significant and substantively important' positive correlation between aid spending: the higher the number of migrants hosted from a particular country, the larger the allocation of aid to the sending country, and

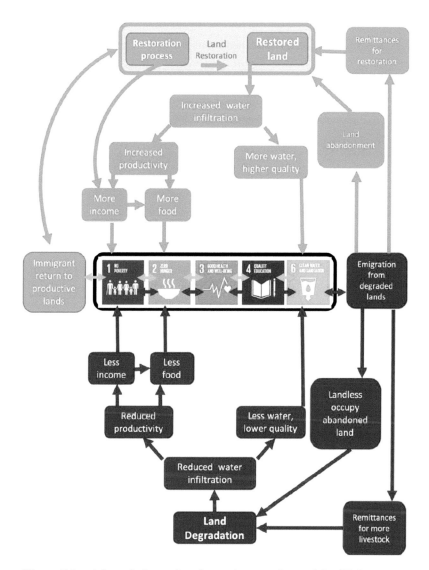

Figure 7 Land degradation, migration and restoration and the SDG nexus.
Negative and positive policy feedback of remittances identified by IRP.
Source: Herrick et al. (2019).

that the levels of spending actually *increased* when migration policies in host States became more restrictive. They suggest this can be explained by both: (i) a desire or expectation on the part of donors that aid funding pacifies some of the driving forces behind migration in countries of net outwards migration, and (ii) the role of diaspora from such locations within host countries in mobilizing/ lobbying for increasing allocations of aid resources. As the economy grows, migration can also grow and then can eventually decline. The diaspora can also have more mobile habitation between country of origin and migration, particularly near retirement.

The findings of Lanati and Thiele (2018) statistical analysis of the relationship between overseas development assistance (ODA) and levels of migration appear to further reinforce this suggestion. They 'obtain evidence of a negative relationship between ODA spending and emigration rates' seemingly even in the case of disaster related to natural hazards (a conclusion shared by Beine & Parsons, 2015). An important concept to consider in this regard is the migrant labour dependency ratio, the extent to which the domestic population is dependent on migrant labour. It is calculated by dividing the domestic population not working by the migrant population that have migrated outside for work. A high total dependency ratio indicates a scarcity of workers to support both the young and the elderly, either directly or through the tax system. Conversely, a low dependency ratio implies that a large number of working age people exist at origin, which increases the likelihood of emigration. In Lanati and Thiele's analysis both effects are significant for the full sample but turn insignificant at conventional levels when running separate regressions for richer and poorer countries.

Research shows that donor policies related to migration in source countries need to carefully be attenuated to specific conditions and be adaptable to particular dependency demographics. Another intriguing resource nexus to such migrant flows that is spurred by labour supply is the scale and scope of agricultural migrant workers worldwide – particularly from Central America to the United States. Despite a rise in automation, there is still considerable reliance on migrant workers in specific agricultural sectors such as food and vegetable horticulture. Human mobility patterns and policies that allow for such labour movements are thus essential for food resource security.

3 Governing Mobility amidst Ecological Disasters and Disruptive 'Attractors'

Human displacements caused by war, famine, and other disasters were recognized as key areas of international engagement when the League of Nations was formed in the early twentieth century following the massive global trauma of World War I. At the Paris Peace Conference in 1920, there was a stark realization for the need to coordinate the massive influx of refugees and the Norwegian explorer, and polymath Fridtjof Nansen was appointed as the High Commissioner for Refugees in 1921, a position which won him the Nobel Peace Prize a year later. Following his sudden death in 1930, the League

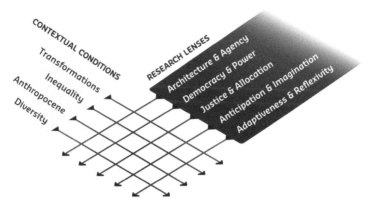

Figure 8 Adaptiveness and reflexivity in the science plan for the earth systems governance project.
Source: Earth Systems Governance (2022).

established the Nansen International Office for Refugees, which itself won a Nobel Peace Prize in 1938. The Nansen name's legacy in dealing with the current migration challenge was embodied in the establishment of the Nansen Initiative on Disaster Displacement in 2012. Through a deliberative process the initiative considered ways in which natural hazards induced migration could be better managed at the international level. After several years of activity, the Nansen Initiative officially became the Platform on Disaster Displacement (PDD) in 2016 with a permanent secretariat in Geneva.

Among the key features of an earth systems governance approach is the 'adaptiveness' that is embedded in the overall functioning the socio-ecological interface (Siebenhüner et al., 2021). Major environmental disasters can lead to temporary or long-term displacement, and an earth systems lens allows us to navigate such eventualities with multiple criteria as shown in Figure 8.

The PDD defines its mandate as 'situations where people are forced to leave their homes or places of habitual residence as the result of a disaster or in order to avoid the impact of an immediate and foreseeable natural hazard'. In 2020, more than 30 million people were newly displaced by disasters (IDMC, 2021).[4] When assessed against environmental predictions, it is not unrealistic to expect that the frequency and severity of extreme weather events owing to climate change, and the societal, economic, and resource pressures that these create, will continue to be accountable for a notable movement of people in coming years and decades. The Nansen Initiative and the subsequent Global PDD will be examined in this section as a potential

---

[4] www.internal-displacement.org/research-areas/Displacement-disasters-and-climate-change.

template for earth systems governance of stochastic events such as earth-quakes and volcanic eruptions as well as events accelerated by anthropogenic climate change.

The PDD is a State-led initiative working towards better protection for persons displaced across borders in the context of disasters and climate change. Established in July 2016, the PDD continues the work of its predecessor – the Swiss and Norwegian led Nansen Initiative – by supporting States and other stakeholders to strengthen protection and to prevent or reduce disaster displace-ment risks. Its main goal is to support the implementation of the Nansen Initiative's Agenda for the Protection of Cross-Border Displaced Persons in the Context of Disasters and Climate Change (Protection Agenda). The Protection Agenda offers States a toolbox for responding to disaster displace-ment. Endorsed by 109 States in 2015, it identifies three priority areas for action: collecting data and enhancing knowledge; enhancing the use of humani-tarian protection measures for cross-border disaster-displaced persons; and strengthening the management of disaster displacement risk in the country of origin. The latter may entail integrating human mobility challenges within disaster risk reduction and climate change action strategies; facilitating migra-tion with dignity as a potential way to cope with natural hazards and adverse effects of climate change; improve planned relocation as a preventative or responsive measure to disaster and displacement risk; and ensuring that the needs of IDPs in disaster situations are specifically addressed.

The PDD seeks to bring together States and other stakeholders in supporting and implementing the recommendations of the Protection Agenda. With the aim of facilitating the exchange of knowledge and strengthening of capacity to prevent, reduce, and address disaster displacement, the PDD supports national, regional, and international efforts to address disaster displacement from different angles, including climate change action, disaster risk reduction, humanitarian protection and assistance, migration governance, and so on. It also provides practical assist-ance and technical support, and acts as a knowledge-sharing and advocacy plat-form across relevant policy and action areas and stakeholder groups.

Beyond the Protection Agenda, the PDD supports the implementation of the Sendai Framework for Disaster Risk Reduction (DRR) 2015–30, the Paris Agreement under the United Nations Framework Convention on Climate Change (UNFCCC) and the Global Compacts for Migration (GCM), and on Refugees (GCR), at the regional level. In cooperation with a multitude of partners – including governments, the UN, international and regional organiza-tions, academia, and civil society – the PDD works to consolidate and enhance the use of effective practices and promote policy coherence. The Sendai Framework for Disaster Risk Reduction presents an opportunity to consider

Table 2 Priorities and guiding principles of the Sendai framework for disaster risk reduction

Priorities for Action

There is a need for focused action within and across sectors by States at local, national, regional, and global levels in the following four priority areas.

Priority 1	Priority 2	Priority 3	Priority 4
Understanding disaster risk	Strengthening disaster risk governance to manage disaster risk	Investing in disaster risk reduction for resilience	Enhancing disaster preparedness for effective response, and to 'Build Back Better' in recovery, rehabilitation and reconstruction
Disaster risk management needs to be based on an understanding of disaster risk in all its dimensions of vulnerability, capacity, exposure of persons and assets, hazard characteristics, and the environment	Disaster risk governance at the national, regional and global levels is vital to the management of disaster risk reduction in all sectors and ensuring the coherence of national and local frameworks of laws, regulations and public policies that, by defining roles and responsibilities, guide, encourage and incentivize the public and private sectors to take action and address disaster risk	Public and private investment in disaster risk prevention and reduction through structural and non-structural measures are essential to enhance the economic, social, health and cultural resilience of persons, communities, countries and their assets, as well as the environment. These can be drivers of innovation, growth, and job creation. Such measures are cost-effective and instrumental to save lives, prevent and reduce losses and ensure effective recovery and rehabilitation	Experience indicates that disaster preparedness needs to be strengthened for more effective response and ensure capacities are in place for effective recovery. Disasters have also demonstrated that the recovery, rehabilitation and reconstruction phase, which needs to be prepared ahead of the disaster, is an opportunity to 'Build Back Better' through integrating disaster risk reduction measures. Women and persons with disabilities should publicly lead and promote gender-equitable and universally accessible approaches during the response and reconstruction phases

Guiding Principles

Primary responsibility of States to prevent and reduce disaster risk, including through cooperation	Shared responsibility between central Government and national authorities, sectors, and stakeholders as appropriate to national circumstances	Protection of persons and their assets while promoting and protecting all human rights including the right to development	Engagement from all of society	Full engagement of all State institutions of an executive and legislative nature at national and local levels	Empowerment of local authorities and communities through resources, incentives, and decision-making responsibilities as appropriate	Decision-making to be inclusive and risk-informed while using a multi-hazard approach
Coherence of disaster risk reduction and sustainable development policies, plans, practices and mechanisms, across different sectors	Accounting of local and specific characteristics of disaster risks when determining measures to reduce risk	Addressing underlying risk factors cost-effectively through investment versus relying primarily on post-disaster response and recovery	'Build Back Better' for preventing the creation of, and reducing existing, disaster risk	The quality of global partnership and international cooperation to be effective, meaningful and strong	Support from developed countries and partners to developing countries to be tailored according to needs and priorities as identified by them	

Source: UNDRR (2022)

approaches of operationalizing earth systems governance, as shown in Table 2. However, there are still features of the Sendai framework's guiding principles which follow a traditionalist mode State-centred responsibility. Human mobility and migration as an adaptive strategy within this framework is a socio-ecological adaptation strategy.

While still in its early phase, the PDD has engaged in policy formation and negotiation in several regions of the world:

– In the Pacific region, the PDD is currently working on the Pacific Response to Disaster Displacement (PRDD) project, in collaboration with the Internal Displacement Monitoring Centre (IDMC), the IOM and European Union (EU). This project is supporting governments in planning for, preventing and responding to disaster displacement. It focuses on the collection, analysis, and dissemination of disaster displacement risk data, the development of policies and frameworks addressing human mobility challenges, and the development of country-specific tools to strengthen the operational preparedness and response capacity of governments in participating countries.

– It is also engaged in work in West Africa, alongside IOM and the UN Office of the High Commissioner for Refugees (UNHCR), to support States in West Africa in their efforts to minimize displacement and facilitate regular migration pathways in the context of disasters, climate change, and environmental degradation. This project supports the implementation of State commitments as set out in the GCM and the African Union Three-Year Implementation Plan of Action for the GCM in Africa 2020–2, among others.

– In Eastern Africa, The Free Movement Protocol for the Intergovernmental Authority on Development (IGAD) Region (Sudan, South Sudan, Ethiopia, Eritrea, Djibouti, Somalia, Kenya, and Uganda) explicitly addresses disaster displacement and at present, PDD is involved in a Multi-Partner Trust Fund project in partnership with IOM, the International Labour Organization (ILO), UNHCR, IGAD, and the IGAD Climate Prediction and Application Centre (ICPAC). As well as building the capacity of national government officials to be better prepared when responding to disaster displacement, it will contribute to facilitating pathways for regular migration in the IGAD region and minimizing displacement risk in the context of climate change, environmental degradation and disasters.

– In the Americas, the PDD is working closely with the Regional Conference on Migration (RCM), the South American Conference on Migration (SACM), and their respective member countries to implement regional guidelines on admission and stay in disaster and climate change contexts. This includes supporting the development of national policy guidance on disaster displacement, for example, with the Government of Chile and others. It is complemented by efforts to promote binational and regional simulation exercises to test the applicability of regional guidelines and the development of more specific Standard Operating Procedures on admission and stay.

Despite these accomplishments, the platform will remain challenged to deliver a global safety net for disaster-induced displacement unless there is a move beyond reactive policy solutions. An earth systems governance approach to empowering the PDD would require countries to consider nested hierarchies of responses at multiple scales. Thus, although domestic responses to disaster-induced displacement may well be prioritized over international action, there should be a willingness to coordinate human capital needs in neighbouring countries which allow skilled labour to be prioritized from such disaster-struck regions. An earth systems approach would also consider mechanisms by which data on disaster vulnerability could lead to preventative investment from donors and the private sector to create resilience. For example, learning from multiple recent earthquakes in Haiti, an earth systems approach would not wait until a disaster struck to mobilize aid but rather anticipate the need for infrastructure upgrading and opportunities for more adaptive livelihoods.

Disruptive 'Attractors' and Reform Efforts

Natural resources are partly determined by physical geography – soil, minerals, and water availability can determine what kind of economically viable activity can occur in an area. Physical geography can also lead to clustering of resources in particular areas which can lead to an 'attraction effect' that draws in human populations around the proverbial 'honeypot'. In complex systems discourse there is also the notion of 'attractors', which confer a point of ordered structure in a chaotic system. At a macro-level, resource rushes can provide such structure and symbolize an attractor phenomenon even though at the micro-level a resource rush may seem chaotic in terms of rapid human movement. What resource rushes thus suggest is an opportunity for governance to take route in concentrated human demographic circumstances. There is thus a disruptive elegance to resource rushes which systems scientists should consider in governance analysis.

For renewable resources such as agriculture and forests, water, and climate are the limiting factors which can constrain long-term habitability of human populations near the resource. If the land remains arable and water and climate temperature modalities are within viable ranges, human habitation can continue with each growing season. However, in the case of mineral resources, there are clearly more finite time horizons for human settlement that is related to the resource.

Although some mines such as the mercury mines of Almaden in Spain have lasted for several hundred years, most mines last for only a few decades. Furthermore, minerals can occur in locations where arable land and water may not be readily available and hence human habitation can be constrained. The discovery of mineral deposits, particularly of gemstones and some precious metals can also occur quite dramatically through itinerant miners. In these geographically specific locations, this can lead to 'mineral rushes' and also create a 'boom and bust' human migration trajectory to communities in these regions. Policies around resource rushes have to be fine-tuned to the modalities of these aspects of the mineral economy.

Temporary migrations linked to mineral extraction ventures at the larger scale can also lead to major secondary impacts on resources in remote sites. Historically, 'boom towns' would emerge near these mineral rushes due to rapid migration and the go into rapid decline once the resources were depleted, leading to proverbial 'mining ghost towns'. The Chamber of Minerals and Energy Western Australia (CMEWA) – a region which has seen more than its fair share of such of 'Drive-in-Drive Out' (DIDO) or 'Fly-in-Fly-Out' (FIFO) operations – contend that 'the increase in FIFO employment in recent years has been driven by a tighter and more competitive labour market, increasing volatility in the resources sector, increased disparity between the relatively large construction workforces and smaller operational workforces in new projects, and increased dispersion of resources operations' (Morris, 2012). Specific policies to limit such disruptive cycles of ephemeral migration generally centre around fostering greater and more sustainable localized development of areas adjacent to mining operations, such as providing incentive packages to industry workers to settle more permanently in such communities, and assurances and/or securing of funding for local service and infrastructure development (Morris, 2012).

A Case of Resource Rushes: Formalization of Artisanal Mining

Artisanal and small-scale mining (ASM) tends to occur in impoverished parts of the world where poverty can lead to rapid mineral rushes if deposits of a precious mineral are found. Although estimates vary, there are thought to be 100 million people directly and indirectly engaged in ASM globally in over eighty countries (IGF, 2018). Most of these countries are low-income nations in sub-Saharan Africa, South America, Oceania, and Asia. In many of these countries, ASM is a long-established craft that antedates European contact and colonialism, for instance in the Akan region of Ghana, traditional gold mining was used for the kingdom of Akan. Today ASM has been estimated to account for 80 per cent of global sapphire, 20 per cent of gold mining and up to 20 per cent of diamond extraction. Artisanal and small-scale mining has become linked to global mineral commodity markets. It is heavily criticized for environmental degradation, linkages to smuggling, labour trafficking, money laundering, and intensifying negative social and ecological externalities. Despite this, ASM has been established as a poverty-driven livelihood strategy that attracts a labour force willing to work under hazardous conditions to supplement low incomes. In low-income countries, diminishing agricultural productivity and poverty have been identified as drivers pushing the rural labour force into ASM (Hilson & Garforth, 2012).

Artisanal and small-scale mining's environmental impact is associated with pollution and large-scale deforestation that turn productive and previously intact landscapes into wastelands. Artisanal and small-scale mining in gold mining is notoriously linked to mercury emission with negative impacts on public health and food systems. An estimated one-third of all mercury emissions are generated by ASM worldwide (Telmer & Veiga, 2009). This is in addition to its other numerous environmental impacts. Alluvial gemstone mining in countries such as our case study of Madagascar's sapphire rush towns attracts artisanal and small-scale miners. The geographic location of mineral and gemstone deposits close to protected lands and farmlands is noteworthy and illustrates potential land-use conflicts.

The scale and speed of these rushes can be highly anarchic and in the absence of clear governance mechanisms, the migration of miners can lead to considerable resource impact in sensitive environments. The UK government and the University of Dundee have distilled a series of recommendations to formalize ASM activities, which can in turn lead to more effective management policies around such mineral rushes. Some of these key policy recommendations are summarized next.

1. Revised and Improved Licensing Processes

Nearly every country with any notable level of ASM activity has licensing systems for the sector. Yet, without exception, the vast majority of artisanal mining operations continue to work in an unlicensed and transient fashion outside of legal frameworks and regulations. While the dynamics behind this trend vary by context, in simple terms most ASM remains informal because of there is little incentive to formalize: obtaining a licence is typically an outdated, overly costly and/or bureaucratic (and in some cases corrupt) process: due to a lack of governmental outreach there is little chance of being caught and punished for operating illegally: and, for the same reason, those who do operate legally get little in return in terms of assistance and assurances. Streamlining the licensing process by making it faster, affordable, accessible (such as decentralizing the process and brining it online) and locally appropriate can help significantly with formalization.

2. Access to Land and Information

One of the most prevalent issues for more regulated ASM is a lack of access to or availability of land that is economically viable for ASM (Hilson & Maponga, 2004). Without such information, artisanal miners are much more likely to opportunistically prospect on agricultural land, conservation areas, or encroach on large-scale mining concessions, increasing the mobility of people operating in a typically environmentally destructive manner. Conducting, or releasing existing data on, geological prospecting and demarcating land specifically for ASM would significantly help address alleviate this trend, providing miners with more permanence to their activities and discouraging transient mining practices. Large-scale mining companies have been encouraged in many locations to cede areas of land that they are not planning to exploit for working by artisanal miners instead. Much more action is needed on this front, as are additional initiatives by authorities to independently allocate areas for ASM.

3. Education, Training, and Assistance

Challenging in the fact that it is something that is probably required for formalization to be conducted effectively yet in many contexts cannot be justifiably delivered (in a legal and/or logistical sense) to informal miners. But certainly, education and training can encourage better mining practice, as evidenced by outreach done through, for example, the Global Mercury Project (Huidobro et al., 2006; McDaniels et al., 2010). Developing accessible and appropriate technical and vocational education and training resources for miners should aim to include information on safe working practices, in terms of both health and safety and the environment, coupled with more effective mining techniques. This is in order to reduce the negative social and environmental impacts of operations and improve working conditions, yields and, consequently, incomes.

4. Supporting Miners 'in the Field'

Developing and maintaining support facilities for miners to attend in order to receive and exchange information, lease or purchase good quality equipment, and refine and process ores are something that has long been advocated but extremely rarely implemented effectively in practice (see Amoah & Stemn, 2018). As with broader community interventions, it is essential that the needs of miners and dependents are properly assessed to ensure such support facilities meet their requirements and local contexts. Creating central hubs of mining activity might also consolidate settlement of miners to more limited geographical areas.

5. Improved Institutional Capacity

As implied in the previous points, the informality of the ASM sector is not simply a wilful avoidance of formal channels and regulations. Rather, much of it stems from a lack of outreach from mandated authorities to assist and enforce. Typically, in mineral-rich lower income countries where ASM is at its most prevalent, the artisanal mining governance comes as more or less an afterthought to regulation of the large-scale mining sector (Hilson & McQuilken, 2014). A long overdue strengthening of government departments and institutions, encouraging effective collaboration and coordination of different ministries and departments at both the national and local level will be essential for any meaningful formalization of ASM.

6. Better Monitoring and Enforcement

Extending from the above points and those preceding it, manpower and various resources available to artisanal mining regulators are, without exception, woefully inadequate to effectively perform their roles (Clifford, 2014). There needs to be a significantly increased capacity of government agencies to better monitor and consistently enforce ASM activities, on the one hand, and assist miners with training, education, and compliance and build positive working relationships, on the other. Ensuring artisanal mining is confined to designated areas and using best practice reduces the transience of the sector and offers more protection to the degradation of surrounding resources like agricultural lands and water catchment systems.

7. Revision and Formulation of Policies Specifically for the ASM Sector

In addition to being poorly enforced, ASM regulations in many countries are outdated and inappropriate, having been formulated during much earlier policymaking consultations with the multilateral or bilateral partners, or having been modelled on large-scale processes or imported verbatim from other countries, respectively. A new period of consideration is certainly required to ensure that existing laws and regulations are still functional, feasible and sufficiently in tune with ASM activities and local contexts.

8. Improve the Involvement of ASM Associations and Cooperatives

Any attempt to successfully drive formalization and its associated reforms highlighted above should, of course, involve coordination with artisanal miners expected to comply. This poses a significant challenge in many contexts, such as sub-Saharan Africa, because artisanal mining is often transient and unorganized. However, in other locations such as South America, a longer-standing tradition of collective action has seen the formation of well-organized ASM associations that have been beneficial to miners and policymakers alike: they provide a single entity with which to engage and consult on matters and a forum for the exchange of knowledge. Encouraging more widespread organization and representation of ASM communities would be a significant advantage to formalization processes.

While the example of ASM might intuitively appear to be relatively specialized, we can also imagine contexts where resources other than metals and minerals may encourage migration and consequent pressure on and competition with other resource uses; a poorly managed expansion of agricultural land use in a previously unutilized area, for example. Here, we might see the same movement of people seeking to take the opportunity to use these resources, and a struggle to effectively oversee and legislate for this new development depending upon the context.

4 Adaptive Governance on Migration due to Climate Change or Resource Needs

Human mobility is an important adaptive strategy to accommodate around a range of economic and ecological stressors. Rural–urban migration and mineral resource rushes are examples of the 'honeypot' phenomenon, but they can also foster long-term resilience if appropriately governed. Paradigms of adaptive governance such as 'managed retreat' of human populations in coastal areas also provides an opportunity for operationalizing earth systems governance. Migration presents a key manifestation of what earth systems governance theorists refer to as the 'Anthropocene gap' in contemporary political structures at the domestic and international level. The sheer scale of human impacts on the planet in terms of both ecological degradation and economic inequality have made existing governance mechanisms largely ineffective. Furthermore, migration has itself been weaponized by rogue elements and resources could potentially also be used as levers in creating conditions for displacement. In her pioneering study *Weapons of Mass Migration: Forced Displacement, Coercion, and Foreign Policy*, Kelly Greenhill (2010) considered at least fifty-six cases of what she called 'coercive engineered migrations' since 1951. She found that progenitors of such interventions achieved their goals in 73 per cent of these cases and virtually all of its goals in over half (57 per cent). In this milieu, the need for adaptive strategies to dealing with such rogue elements who could manipulate resource factors becomes even more acute.

Disaster-Induced Temporary and Permanent Migration Policies

Since 1990, the United States has granted a form of humanitarian relief called Temporary Protected Status (TPS) to nationals of certain countries that have become embroiled in violent conflict or suffered a natural hazard. An estimated 340,000 people currently hold TPS status. As its name implies, TPS is not a grant of permanent legal status in the United States. Recipients do not receive lawful permanent residence (a green card), nor are they eligible, based on their TPS status, to apply for permanent residence or for US citizenship. Rather, TPS beneficiaries receive provisional protection against deportation and permission to work in the United States for a limited period of time. The United States can end a country's TPS designation once it has recovered from the triggering event.

Congress created TPS in 1990 to establish a uniform system for granting temporary protection to people unable to return to their home countries because of a political or environmental catastrophe. Before 1990, the executive branch dealt with this scenario by designating certain countries for Extended Voluntary Departure (EVD), an administrative status that amounted to an exercise of prosecutorial discretion by the Attorney General not to pursue nationals of certain countries for removal if found to be living in the United States without authorization. However, there were no established criteria explaining how a country might qualify for EVD, and critics alleged that decisions regarding the grant of EVD to nationals of a particular country were often politically motivated. This argument became especially prominent in the late 1980s, when the Reagan administration decided not to designate El Salvador for EVD despite the country's ongoing civil war.

To resolve the controversy, Congress created TPS, a statutory mechanism for granting protection against deportation to nationals of designated countries. Under current law, the Homeland Security Secretary may designate a country for TPS when one of three circumstances occurs:

(a) There is 'ongoing armed conflict' that creates unsafe conditions for returning nationals;
(b) There has been an earthquake, flood, drought, epidemic, or other environmental disaster that makes the State temporarily unable to accept the return of its nationals, and the State has requested TPS designation; or
(c) 'Extraordinary and temporary' conditions in a State prevent its nationals from returning safely.

Once a country has been designated for TPS, its nationals who are residing in the United States at the time of the designation may be granted protection if they meet certain criteria. These include having been continuously present in the United States as of a date specified by the Department of Homeland Security and having a relatively clean criminal record. Individuals who are granted TPS receive two main benefits: a reprieve from deportation and authorization to work. TPS holders may also apply for special permission to travel internationally and return to the United States. Temporary Protected Status does *not* confer permanent residency, citizenship, or any right to ongoing immigration status (Messick and Bergeron, 2014).[5]

Though marginally restrictive in its criteria, support mechanisms, and intended longevity, through numbers alone, TPS is the one of (if not the) largest temporary displacement mechanisms worldwide. Debates have been raised about the number of designated countries eligible for TPS and the length of times that people can reside in the United States (Wilson, 2020). There is certainly a justifiable argument that the definitions and associated criteria for claiming might also be re-evaluated in light of emerging understandings of the role of longer-term, more subtle, accumulative processes in creating acute resource pressures, rather than considering 'disaster' events alone.

Managed Retreat Policies

Managed retreat policies and approaches can be thought of as 'the purposeful, coordinated movement of people and assets out of harm's way' (Carey, 2020). While by no means a new concept for human societies, the predicted pervasiveness of slow environmental change in the modern context indicates that it is highly likely that more people are going to have to move, and on a longer-term (to permanent) basis. Additionally, with the contemporary availability of climatic data and modelling, many modern retreat policies are being derived proactively rather than purely reactively.

Coastal Retreat Strategies

Coastal environs and their communities, being some of the most vulnerable locations worldwide for degradation of land and resources, are at comparatively advanced stages in terms of managed retreat planning, conceptually and empirically. Georgetown University's Climate Centre outlines several measures and regulatory tools, which can be used individually or in combination, for managed

---

[5] www.migrationpolicy.org/article/temporary-protected-status-united-states-grant-humanitarian-relief-less-permanent.

retreat in coastal areas: such efforts are also well-aligned with the growing policy literature on 'nature-based solutions'.

Living Shorelines: Traditional approaches to protect coastal development from flooding and erosion have focused on 'hard armouring' – physical infrastructure like seawalls and breakwaters. Increasingly, however, coastal States and communities are turning towards 'living shorelines' or 'soft armouring' techniques, such as dune creation and wetland restoration. As well as preserving many of the biodiversity and aesthetic components of coastal environments, this latter approach also avoids the more 'explosive' negative impacts of hard armouring structures which can rapidly flood and erode surrounding properties and beaches they fail or are breached.

Setback and Buffers: A setback is a mandated distance that a structure must be located behind a baseline location, like a tidal line, or a natural protective feature like coastal dunes, wetland, or floodplain. In a similar fashion, buffers and buffer zones place restrictions on property development to preserve important natural protective functions.

Development Permit Conditions: Involves placing longer-term conditions on coastal property development, with the expectation from both government and civilians that development will likely eventually have to relocate due to future coastal change. Levels of government might legislate in coastal management and/or zoning codes that existing and planned properties must relocate if compromised by certain events such as beach or cliff erosion or permanent shifts in tidal lines.

Zoning and Overlays: Similar to above, local governments can consider using zoning and overlay zones to support a variety of goals related to managed retreat, including phasing out or reducing development in vulnerable coastal areas, instead attempting to shift density and new development in higher ground areas. Overlay zones or districts can impose additional regulations on an existing zone based on its special characteristics, such as for natural, historical, or cultural resource protection.

The concept of Earth System Governance was born, around 2000, out of the recognition of the need for a fundamental change in the management of global socio-ecological systems to cope with the extraordinary impact of human activities (Biermann, 2007). Early iterations of the concept were centred on the reorientation and restructuring of international institutions (Biermann et al., 2012). More recently it has focused on guiding the systematic study of how societies prepare for accelerated climate change and wider earth system change, as well as policy responses by developing a framework for research into the subject (Burch et al., 2019). This framework is built on a set of themes that cover observations of how the earth system(s) are changing, and a set of research lens for understanding and developing the governance of these changes. In this Element we have explored a variety of ways in which natural resources (as representing the ecological in socio-ecological systems) and migration or mobility (as representing the socio in socio-ecological systems) interact with each other. Drawing a parallel with the new directions of ESG we have shown that the relationship of migration and resources: (i) can be trans-formational in changing livelihoods, and economies; (ii) involves inequalities, such as who moves, who is left behind and who is impacted by changes in resources and migration; (iii) can be complex and emergent in terms of their dynamics and outcomes; and (iv) involves a diversity of interests and know-ledge systems. As advocated with an ESG lens the governance of the nexus of migration and resources needs to be adaptive to these realities. In this section we outline the major governance themes currently of relevance to migration and natural resources.

UNFCCC Loss and Damage Framework

While the UNFCCC recognizes climate-induced migration as an effective adaptation strategy in the 2009 Cancun Adaptation Framework, existing inter-national policy frameworks do not provide sufficient assistance and protection for people moving due to the effects of climate change. For example, the 1951 Geneva Refugee Convention and its 1967 Protocol do not recognize climate change as a reason for granting refugee status. Also at national level, there are hardly any examples of legal frameworks that grant protection to 'climate refugees' and support their relocation in line with their needs. The following international instruments are important in this regard.

• The UNFCCC Task Force on Displacement, created under the Warsaw International Mechanism for Loss and Damage associated with Climate Change Impacts (WIM);
• Regional relevant policy discussions under the Economic Community of West African States (ECOWAS) and the IGAD;
• The Almeria Conference on Desertification and Migration.

In some contexts, it is already the case or highly likely in the immediate future that mitigation efforts have or will fail to prevent continued anthropogenically driven pressures on natural resource stocks and environmental conditions, making adaptation unviable. Vulnerable nations have strongly argued that existing frameworks are inadequate to protect their environmental futures and called for an international mechanism to deal with residual 'loss and damage'. The UNFCCC, which established the WIM in response to such concerns, defines loss and damage as 'the actual and/or potential manifestation of impacts associated with climate change in developing countries that negatively affect human and natural systems'. Yet as Roberts and Andrei (2015) highlight, establishing what is incorporated into these impacts and, centrally, quantifying them is extremely multifaceted:

> Loss and damage that is not avoided is categorized as either economic or non-economic loss and damage. Economic loss and damage – including loss of gross domestic product (GDP) and loss and/or damage to physical assets – is accounted for in formal accounting processes... Non-economic losses such as the loss of lives, traditional or indigenous knowledge, ecosystem services and cultural, social and psychological impacts, are not accounted for in formal accounting process and therefore are more difficult to both measure and address.

The WIM aims to assist developing countries that are particularly vulnerable to the adverse effects of climate change by: enhancing knowledge and understanding of comprehensive risk management approaches to address loss and damage: strengthening dialogue, coordination, coherence, and synergies among relevant stakeholders: and enhancing action and support, including finance, technology and capacity-building (UNFCCC, 2021). Their five 'strategic workstreams' address slow-onset events, non-economic losses, risk management approaches, action and support, and human mobility.

Despite the consensus over the need for loss and damage being rhetorically reaffirmed with the signing of the Paris Agreement in 2015 and discussed at each COP since, the specifics behind mechanisms to deal with both forms (economic and non-economic) loss and damage have proven politically controversial and, consequently, faltering in their conception, development, and policy implementation (Carbon Brief, 2017; Mace & Verheyen, 2016). Unlike the other two 'pillars' of the UNFCCC – mitigation and adaptation – with promised amounts of US$100 billion-a-year in financing, there are currently no clear policy frameworks or sources of funding for or governance over loss and damage. Discussions on the topic that took place at COP26 saw demands from lower- and middle-income States for much more tangible action (Pierre-Nathoniel et al., 2019). The next official review of the WIM has been set for 2024.

Suggestions of any form of reparation between countries are inevitably the source of differing levels of controversy in the international policymaking arena. Yet, logically, the idea that one can hope to address the current and future environmental and resource dynamic – that is, relatively clear consensus on mitigation and adaptation with UNFCCC frameworks – without comprehensively dealing with pre-existing degradation of resources seems questionable. And, if part of our agenda is to prevent forced displacement of people as a result of resource shifts and degradation, appropriately supporting countries beginning from a disadvantaged position in this context would also appear to be a prudent approach.

Towards Mobility Justice within Resource Constraints

As a starting point, the concept of 'mobility justice' provides an overarching framework within which to consider migration and natural resources in terms of social and development policy. Key elements of such a provocative approach have been highlighted by sociologist Mimi Sheller (2018) as follows:

- All people shall enjoy a right to exit and re-enter the territory from which they originate;
- There is a right to refuge for those fleeing violence, persecution, and loss of domicile by war;
- People displaced by climate change shall have a right to resettlement in other countries, especially in those counties that contributed most to climate change; New Zealand's prospect for validating a 'climate passport' for vulnerable island populations may be considered as an example in this regard;
- There is a right to freedom of movement across borders for any temporary purpose defined by law (tourism, education, temporary work);
- No one should be detained or deported without due process;
- Immigration law shall not be used to exclude entire categories of persons on the basis of race, religion, ethnicity, nationality, sexuality or health status.

Having such a foundational ethical framework for policy aspiration can be instructive as policymakers consider more specific operational tenets. Sheller's approach has come under some criticism as well for being Utopian and also disconnected with some of the urgencies of living in the Anthropocene (Baldwin et al., 2019). Migration policies tend to be prompted by economic and employment factors more so than any other variable. Most survey data justify proximate focus on such factors as migrants themselves note the primacy of economic factors in their decisions. For example, a survey conducted by Adger et al. (2021) found that out of a sample size of 1668 migrant respondents in India, Bangladesh, and Ghana, 60 per cent gave economic factors (employment and debt) as primary factors for migration, followed by just under 30 per cent for social factors (education, marriage, health). Only 0.6 per cent (or sixteen individuals) cited environmental motivations (loss of income due to land degradation, extreme events, or loss of seasonal income) for movement.

Indirectly, some of the goals of such a mobility justice framework are also enshrined in major international initiatives. Migration is explicitly mentioned in the following Sustainable Development Goals (SDG) targets, which are important motivators of policy reform as part of the United Nations agenda of planning towards the year 2030:

SDG8 – Target 8.8: 'Protect labour rights and promote safe and secure working environments for all workers, including migrant workers, in particular women migrants, and those in precarious employment'.

SDG 10 – Target 10.7: 'Facilitate orderly, safe, regular, and responsible migration and mobility of people, including through the implementation of planned and well-managed migration policies'.

SDG 10 – Target 10.c: 'By 2030 reduce to less than 3% the transaction costs of migrant remittances and eliminate remittance corridors with costs higher than 5%'.

SDG 17 – Target 17.18: 'By 2030, enhance capacity-building support to developing countries, including for least developed countries and small island developing States (SIDS), to increase significantly the availability of high-quality, timely and reliable data disaggregated by income, gender, age, race, ethnicity, migratory status, disability, geographic location and other characteristics relevant in national contexts'.

Global Compact for Safe, Orderly, and Regular Migration

The Global Compact is framed consistent with target 10.7 of the 2030 Agenda for Sustainable Development in which Member States committed to cooperate internationally to facilitate safe, orderly, and regular migration and its scope is defined in Annex II of the New York Declaration. It is intended to:

- Address all aspects of international migration, including the humanitarian, developmental, human rights-related and other aspects;
- Make an important contribution to global governance and enhance coordination on international migration;
- Present a framework for comprehensive international cooperation on migrants and human mobility;
- Set out a range of actionable commitments, means of implementation and a framework for follow-up and review among Member States regarding international migration in all its dimensions;
- Be guided by the 2030 Agenda for Sustainable Development and the Addis Ababa Action Agenda; and
- Be informed by the Declaration of the 2013 High-Level Dialogue on International Migration and Development.

The subsequent framework set up by the United Nations through the United Nations Migration Network and a range of epistemic bodies lays emphasis on 'evidence-based policy'. There is recognition that human mobility is thus inherently dynamic and complex, and policy must be adaptive based on the most current data being received (Kraly and Hovy, 2020). Some of the points raised by this compact can also be operationalized through regional mechanisms such as the Arctic Council or the Small Island Developing States Accelerated Modalities of Action (SAMOA) pathway for SIDS. There may also be a particular interface in some of these areas with the United Nations Permanent Forum on Indigenous Peoples. There has also been some interest from countries in Scandinavia related to developing a more focused compact on climate-induced migration. New Zealand has also started to work on pre-emptive migration schemes which preferentially allow migration from small island States.

What is missing from the Global Compact is any mechanism which could allow for international regulation of migrant flows and prioritization criteria. As Steven Walt recently observed in an article responding to the migrant crisis in Europe, there is no 'World Migration Organization' akin to the 'World Trade Organization'. The IOM is largely an epistemic organization that provides knowledge products and guidance and support to operational work of relief organizations that intervene post-facto in refugee crises such as UNHCR. What is needed is further sharpening of the Global Compact to elevate its status to at least a treaty which could be enforced at some level through UN auspices. In the meantime, existing environmental treaties, especially, the UNFCCC could engage on key issues that are likely to arise due to global environmental change.

Policies on Climate Mobility Reparations

There are two pathways that can be taken, when it comes to climate reparations. The first is known as 'corrective justice', and refers to a negotiation between governments within an international jurisdiction. Under this scenario, the collective moral responsibility of high greenhouse gas-emitters to make financial recompense to climate creditors forms the legal basis for holding high-emitting States morally accountable for a calculable and bearable share of the harms of climate change. This approach offers a financial mechanism by which the reception of migrants could be handled through an international Green Climate Fund.

Climate reparations between nations would enable 'creditor countries' – such as small island States – to strengthen their resilience by funding disaster risk reduction, insurance, and adaptation to help people remain in place (Burkett, 2015).

One practical mechanism for this would be an international compensation commission, which would receive claims from countries that have incurred adaptation expenses, using as a template the United Nations Claims Commission – which was established after the first Iraq War to handle claims against Iraq for war-related damages.

The second and quite different pathway to climate compensation is through tort litigation for loss and damage against the major fossil fuel companies – in other words, suing the oil companies (a tort is an act or omission that gives rise to injury or harm to another).[6] Through class action lawsuits filed under multiple jurisdictions, reparations could be sought for those harmed by greenhouse gas emissions, and corporations could be held responsible for specific injury, especially if they knew about it and covered it up – a strategy that worked against tobacco companies (e.g. Gottlieb, 1999). In fact, Wewerinke-Singh and Salili (2020) suggest that 'the call for compensation for loss and damage is also supported by well-established rules and principles of international law, including the right to reparations for injury resulting from violations of international law'. According to key legal arguments they issued on behalf of the low-lying and vulnerable country of Vanuatu, the Warsaw International Mechanism for Loss and Damage offers the best opportunity for loss and damage finance, under the auspices of the UNFCCC.

Maladaptation: A Cautionary Note on Adaptive Policies

While typically referring to remediating environmental and resource pressures within socio-environmental systems, it is worth bearing in mind, certainly in a consideration of policymaking, that 'adaptation' (i.e. a process of change in response to an ongoing environmental stimulus) is not intrinsically 'good', either within itself or in relation to a broader context. For climatic or resource concerns, the scope for 'maladaptation' is an area of growing concern. Juhola et al. (2016) defines 'maladaptation' in this sense as 'actions that may lead to increased risk of adverse climate related outcomes, increased vulnerability to climate change, or diminished welfare, now or in the future'. Or, as Schipper (2020) puts and depicts it (Figure 9), we can see maladaptation on one end of a spectrum of potential outcomes where, through inaction or inappropriate action, one drops out of a circular system of positively adapting or coping with ongoing change.

Within the context of climate change, Barnett and O'Neill (2010) suggest five key pathways through which maladaptation can arise, with the final four being highly relevant to the resource and migration nexus:

---

[6] See for example, https://thebulletin.org/2017/10/suing-oil-companies-to-pay-for-climate-change/.

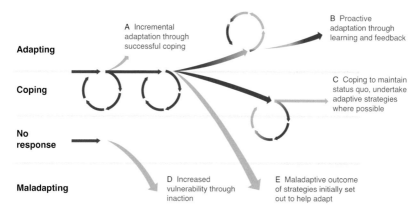

Figure 9 Outcomes spectrum of human dealing with ecological disruption.
Source: Schipper (2020).

(a) Those that increase GHG emissions
(b) Those that disproportionately affect vulnerable groups or populations
(c) Those that have high opportunity costs
(d) Those that reduce the incentive for further adaptation
(e) Those that encourage trajectories that reduce the possibility of adaptation
    for future generations.

Unfortunately, few frameworks currently exist that help better understand and identify the risks and forms of maladaptation. Magnan and Mainguy (2014) combine Barnett and O'Neill's typology within what they call the *Pathways framework* and Hallegatte's (2009) proposed strategies towards climatic uncertainty in their *Precautionary framework* to form an overall assessment framework (Figure 10). They suggest that the eleven 'practice-oriented guidelines' could make a firm basis on which to assess both ex-ante analysis of adaptation initiatives and ex-post evaluations, with the ultimate aim of deriving firmer 'qualified indicators'.

Building on the charge that few integrated frameworks for conceptualizing maladaptation exist, Magnan et al. (2016) suggest that 'despite growing efforts worldwide to adapt to climate change, there appears to be little concern about the risk of maladaptation. There is a real possibility, however, that initiatives taken in the name of adaptation might not only waste financial resources but could also aggravate the consequences of one-off and gradual climate-related changes'. The authors go on to cite case study examples of such concerns in action (also see Eriksen et al., 2021).

Hulhumalé, Maldives: Hulhumalé is an island made of reclaimed land designed to meet the existing and future housing, industrial, and commercial development

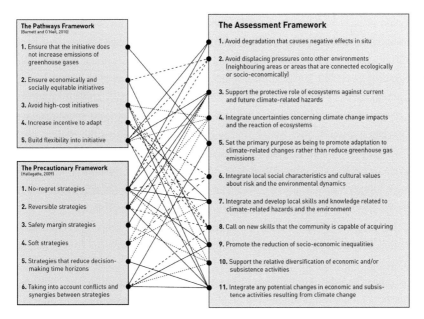

Figure 10 Maladaptation assessment framework.
Source: Magnan and Mainguy (2014).

demands of the Malé region, with the intention of housing between a third and a half of the Maldivian population by 2050. But how viable is this approach longer term? While relocation has and is expected to relieve resource pressures on other parts of the atoll nation, Hulhumalé sits only 2 metres above current sea-level and its creation via extensive dredging has severely damaged surrounding marine ecosystems, including coral reefs.

Afar, Ethiopia: The Afar region is an extensive, arid region of NW Ethiopia where 80 per cent of the population are dependent upon pastoralist livelihoods. Rising temperatures and aridity have severely affected Afar in the past decade. Preference in governmental policy has been towards more 'sustainable' practices, in the form of irrigated, sedentary (often commercial) agriculture. As well as being environmentally problematic in terms of its sustainability considering prevailing conditions, this has intensified resource and social pressures on the decreasing amounts of remaining available land for pastoralists, consequently increasing levels of poverty and conflict, and undermining the ability of groups to adapt to changing conditions.

South-West Bangladesh: An example of, in the authors' words, how 'decision-makers can sometimes justify investments in adaptation on the basis of short- to medium-term benefits, with a high benefit to cost ratio. Over time, as the effects of climate change increase, the benefits can decline, and the investment may have serious adverse consequences'. The multilaterally funded Coastal Climate-Resilient Infrastructure Project in South-West Bangladesh aims to foster climate resilience by upgrading over 500 km of infrastructure and buildings as well as building and improving cyclone and animal shelters. Yet this region is already and will continue to be one of the most vulnerable parts of a country highly susceptible to resource degradation through environmental change. It is suggested that the project may 'insidiously encourage the resident population to remain in these hazardous areas', reduce or reverse the current trends of out-migration from the region, and, over longer temporal ranges, prove unsustainable in its ability to protect the population here from predicted changes in climatic conditions and resource shifts.

The proposed frameworks, conceptual thinking and empirical examples surrounding maladaptation are the potentially ominous side (or 'when things go wrong' as Schipper, 2020 words it) of the same systems approach adopted in this report and the policymaking caveats featured specifically in this section. That is, scholars of maladaptation emphasize the critical importance of considering dynamic, highly contextual drivers of multiple origins over a series of temporal and spatial scales.

Conclusion

The resource nexus with human migration challenges conventional approaches to policymaking because of its inherent properties as a complex adaptive system. The IRP has thus approached this topic at multiple layers where resource drivers and impacts of human mobility are considered as part of a connected system of feedback loops. Since migration can be an adaptive policy for resource constraints and in some cases an inability to migrate can itself cause greater resource stress, linear models and causal theories for policy impact are elusive. An adaptive planning framework is needed with continuous monitoring of a range of data and thresholds. Policymakers need to be flexible in their decision-making approaches and be informed by some of the planning frameworks that are derived from the computational field of operations research. Figure 11 shows a policy-planning framework which could be used in this regard. Further insights on developing an architecture of Earth Systems Governance are now also emerging in the broader literature on the topic (Biermann & Kim, 2020). However, it is essential to operate this at an appropriately focused scale and not be tempted to draw comparisons where the key data parameters are different. The policy-planning process is thus inherently iterative. The goal in the context of our resource nexus with mobility can be measured in terms of efficient resource delivery for a specific target of human well-being, which could be measured through a variety of life quality indices.

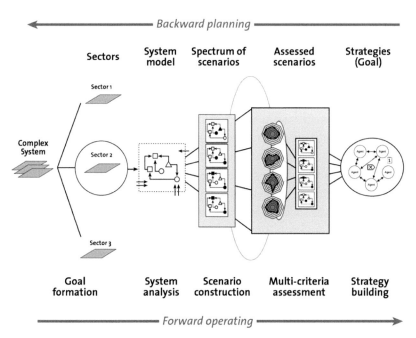

Figure 11 Iterative policy planning for a complex adaptive system.
Source: Wiek and Walter (2009).

The most ecologically efficient resource consumption patterns that are informed by a separate set of policy decisions can then be mapped to those indicators.

Thus, we could envisage a situation where a systems model suggests certain levels of resource scarcity under a range of scenarios. These scenarios could then be considered through a multiple criteria assessment process through a consultative process with local members to come up with contingency plans for voluntary and involuntary mobility. Donors could also glean from such an approach as noted by Ramalingam (2013) in his book *Aid in the Age of Chaos.* While such an iterative approach may be initially unsettling for policymakers, the migration–resource nexus demands such malleability. The use of 'FREE heuristics' or policy and decision-making aiming to be Flexible, Robust, Economic No/Low Regrets and Equitable (FREE) has also been proposed in some contexts (Audia et al., 2021). Through this concluding section we have attempted to provide specific examples of policy tools which could be used in a range of qualitatively diffuse scenarios involving resources and human mobility. Duit et al. (2010) argue that 'at the end of the day, governance solutions for many of those problems rooted in complex systems dynamics will, as always, consist in incrementally implemented, heterogenic, and piecemeal mixes of policy instruments, institutions, networks and organizations'.

The ESG approach provides us an opportunity to consider adaptive mechanisms of governing migration, which many conventional approaches cannot accommodate. Biermann (2010) sets forth some key features of this approach that are well-aligned with the challenges that are evident when linking natural resources to human mobility. There is an intergenerational dependency dimension to this approach that is well suited to the migration discourses as the decisions of a social group to move can create diasporas that impacts the natural resource nexus over long timescales. There is also functional interdependency where this refers 'to the interdependence of natural subsystems – linking, for instance, climate change to biodiversity or land degradation – as well as to the interdependence of social systems and policy areas' (Bierman, 2010, p. 66). Migration impacts other and natural resources clearly have interdependent impacts which can be measured and monitored through earth systems governance approaches.

Spatial interdependence is another key feature of ESG approaches. Resources in one area compared to another influence movement and create spatial corridors and connections that need to be governed. Furthermore, an 'extraordinary degree of harm' is possible with a collapse in natural capital from not managing the migration–resource nexus, as demonstrated by resource rushes and boom/bust cycles.

Biermann (2010) outlines four core principles of governance that are needed to develop earth systems approaches:

(a) *Legitimacy and credibility for governments and other stakeholders to believe in a reciprocity of interaction partners over time and space:* In the case of migration this may be operationalized through a reciprocal duty of care around forced displacement from natural resource crises.

(b) *Stability over decades to withstand political changes in participating countries or changes in the world political system:* The Refugee Act and arguably the Guiding Principles for Internally Displaced People have endured such stability but both need to be more explicit about natural resources.

(c) *Adaptiveness as defined as the need to respond quickly to new scientific findings and new interest constellations:* The migration rushes for rare metals needed for time-sensitive transitions for renewable technologies exemplify such an adaptive need.

(d) *Inclusiveness in ways that methods and mechanisms are perceived by all stakeholders as legitimate, effective, and fair:* In the context of migration the growing literature on 'mobility justice' (Sheller, 2020) resonates with the ESG literature on 'planetary justice' (Kashwan et al., 2020).

The planetary boundaries framework encourages researchers and policy-makers to approach governance as a legal framework that must regulate and manage a world to ensure that humanity does not cross or endangers its earthly natural resources required for its healthy survival. The notion of planetary boundaries has brought complex debates and criticism into the study of earth system services and earth system governance (Biermann et al., 2020). In relation to this debate, planetary justice presents a solution on how to smoothen out some of these clashes while putting global governance into legal practice. By placing justice on a planetary scale, questions related to global environmental resource stress, human (im)mobility and systematic resource exploitation of our earth systems are framed as issues linking to human equity, protection and well-being rather than resource politics (Biermann & Kalfagianni, 2020; Dirth et al., 2020).

It is clear that the values and meanings of 'justice' differs in between stakeholders, country governments and even within societies or between human beings, but the framework provides an opportunity to understand justice as concept placed to manage radical transformations of our earth system. It brings structure and helps clarify or refocus the aims and needs of global governance. The framing also supports in reducing power, political and financial imbalances, and exploitation of resources leading to human suffering (Biermann & Kalfagianni, 2020). It also offers a clear steppingstone towards how to practically implement and put the SDG or 'global governance through goals' into national use (Biermann et al., 2017; De Santo et al., 2019; van der Hel & Biermann, 2017).

Building on the earth system governance literature, van der Hel and Biermann (2017) identify three areas of concern related to the creation of the SDGs and UNs attempts to address the conservation and sustainable resource use of biodiversity beyond national borders. These include the following:

(a) The politicization of science and coping with scientific uncertainty,
(b) Institutional fragmentation,
(c) The need for a new agreement to respond to the complex set of multiple, multilevel, and systemic threats to biodiversity (particularly marine) beyond national jurisdiction.

The Anthropocene has forced us to rethink global governance to be able to improve its effectiveness in our intertwined socio-ecological world. This includes both global policy frameworks such as in the context of human (im)mobility the Global Compact for Migration, as well as the way that national laws are built up and operate within countries. To avoid legal separation 'Earth System Law' has been put forward as providing a potential solution that encourages greater collaboration and co-leaning between stakeholders (Kotzé et al., 2022).

All of Biermann (2010) elements as well as later writings such as (Bierman et al, 2019) have the potential for being realized through the Global Compact for Safe, Orderly, and Regular Migration, which acknowledges environmental changes as root causes of migration (Objective 2). Although emphasis within environmental migration scholarship has been placed on its climatic dimensions, it also offers a space to fully acknowledge the importance of natural resources and their management as contributing to the multi-causality of migration and, likewise, the impacts of migration on the environment and natural resources. Earth Systems Governance has seldom been explicitly connected to the implementation of the Global Compacts despite their congruence (van der Vliet & Biermann, 2022). The GCM in particular offers an opportunity to anchor resource dimensions in the international migration governance agenda through the aforementioned core principles of the ESG framework: *credibility, stability, adaptiveness,* and *inclusiveness*. The Global Compacts are based on multi-stakeholder participation, involving governments as well as international organizations, and development institutions in the political terrain of migration and forced displacement: the GCM aims to foster 'international cooperation among all relevant actors on migration, acknowledging that no State can address migration alone' (para 8). This coalesces with the ESG framework's first core principle of governance emphasizing the reciprocity of interactions amongst partners. Here, government and non-government resource stakeholders may be brought into discussions, implementation, and the evaluation of the progress of the GCM such as the four-yearly International Migration Review Forum and in the UN Network for Migration, tasked with enabling effective and coherent system-wide support to the GCM's implementation, follow-up, and review (paras 45, 49).

The Compact is the first time the world has adopted a comprehensive agreement on migration, making way for the beginning for the global regulation of migration (McAdam, 2019). However, the stability of the GCM may be a key factor in determining whether it will fulfil its promise over time. As Biermann (2007: 331) notes, 'governments that commit resources within a global normative framework in the present must rely on the perseverance of this framework over time', which may prove difficult given the political tension and changing public opinions around migration and forced displacement and global shifts in resource demands, availability, and access.

While the GCM will have to rely on the credibility and stability of governance structures to fulfil its promise, at the same time ESG also underlines the need for adaptiveness in governance that responds to new situations. The effective global management of safe, orderly, and regular migration requires that policies consider and adapt to emerging data and evidence and changing socio-economic and political conditions for – including how changes in the global resource landscape (e.g. the impacts of the Russian invasion of the Ukraine) may impact migration flows if governments are to meet the stated objective of minimizing the adverse drivers and structural factors that force people to leave their homes. Including resource governance more explicitly as a cause as underpinning certain migration flows may thus help the GCM boost its claims of 'offer[ing] a 360-degree vision' (para 11).

Lastly, bringing resource considerations and actors into the GCM process helps to fulfil the final ESG governance principle of inclusiveness 'the interdependence of earth system governance, as well as the complexity and uncertainty of the entire system that may change the overall interest constellation within a few years, require the governance system to be as inclusive as possible regarding the stakeholders involved' (Biermann 2007: 331). Considering the importance of South-South migration flows broadly and those linked to resources, specifically, requires a strong emphasis on the participation of low-income countries, but also a participatory, rights-based, and social equity-oriented approach acknowledging the critical role of non-State actors including migrants and other affected populations. Ensuring all parties see the Global Compact for Migration as legitimate, effective, and fair, may prove a particularly difficult task.

5 Key Messages and Interface with United Nations International Resource Panel's Assessment

This Element is part of a larger effort undertaken by the authors for the United Nations International Resource Panel to consider key insights on governance interventions. The relationship between natural resources and migration requires us to consider human-environment interactions as a complex adaptive system. Key properties of such systems suggest that direct causal relationships between resource scarcity and human mobility will remain elusive. Resources can be an intervening variable between global environmental change, including climatic change, and human mobility. This means that resource scarcity measurements can provide early warning with reference to what impact global change may have on proximate indicators of migration. Minerals, arable land, water and energy delivery are the key resource drivers of human mobility. Property rights to these resources as well as opportunities for international migrant remittance flows can be key determinants of migrant decision pathways.

Ten key lessons from the broader analysis to which this Element is anchored are provided in this section:

(1) Natural resources mediate the impacts between global environmental change process and human mobility dynamics. However, the relationship is not linear and can be bidirectional. The linkage between climatic change

and migration deserves particular caution in policy delineation as there is high variability in such prospects by geography and adaptive ability of populations.

The idea of 'environmental mobility' as a result of natural hazards ('rapid change' events) and/or more gradual environmental perturbations ('slow-onset' changes) is one that is becoming increasingly familiar within policymaking circles and in the popular imagination. When dealt with in an unnuanced fashion, observed or predicted environmental changes have been used to create relatively alarmist projections about the potential scale of movement of people, typically from poorer to richer parts of the globe. This can feed into (often quite negative) broader civic and political discussions surrounding migration. There has been an emergence of more in-depth appreciation of how environmental changes and resource pressures might influence migration since the turn of the millennium. It is, however, still anticipated that prevalent diminishment and degradation of various types of resources and ecosystems services that we see occurring across the world is likely to become a more significant influencer on migration trends in the coming century.

Our survey of the existing research and our own presentation of data reaffirm the notion that connections between climate change, resource degradation and movement of people are, however, far from linear (i.e. more change does not necessarily equate to more movement). Messages that make this assumption tend to subvert the growing body of empirical studies that point to both the multi-causal nature of migration and the indirect, 'messier' link between environmental changes of various kinds and the motivations towards and levels of mobility. The dynamics – forms, drivers, processes, and impacts – surrounding both migration and resources are extremely multifaceted. Unsurprisingly, so are the relationships between them.

Such complex and interconnected relationships certainly have an influence on the different 'types' of mobility/migration that we observe occurring: for example, if people move permanently or temporarily, internally or internationally, and whether this mobility is 'chosen' or 'forced'. They can also result in outcomes that can seem superficially counterintuitive: for example, the rejection of migration by the citizens of environmentally threatened SIDS, low mobility from other environmentally vulnerable regions as populations become 'trapped', or the ability of migration to actually *improve* resources in areas of both outwards and inwards migration.

(2) Hydropower infrastructure presents the most direct example of a resource development linkage to involuntary migration.

Using geospatial data, we show that international migrant flows exhibit some evidence of associations with natural resource use. On a regional level, these connections can often be seen much more directly: for example, our work estimates that the top 200 recent hydropower developments (2000–18) have displaced between 900,000 and 2 million people and induced substantial land-use change since the start of the century. We also highlight that refugee camp establishment show characteristics of rapid but both positive (e.g. subsistence farming) and negative (e.g. deforestation) resource and land-use changes.

After selecting 279 hydroelectric dams constructed between 2000 and 2018 from the Global Reservoir and Dam database version 1.3 (2019), we combined all dam points with associated reservoirs, land cover maps and population datasets to estimate environmental and human population changes following dam construction and reservoir filling. The population at risk of displacement was estimated by using the reservoir extent to calculate the total population residing in the area at the time.

There was a 35 per cent increase in the size of water bodies at dam locations between 2000 and 2018, likely attributable to reservoir filling for electricity generation. During the same time, we estimated an 18 per cent decrease in tree cover, likely due to reservoir clearance and filling. China's Three Gorges Dam and two other dams, Brazil's Luis Eduardo and Ethiopia's Gilgel Gibe III dams stand out with visible population changes around dam reservoirs between 2000 and 2020. Still, only the Three Gorges dam showed a decrease in population. The dam with a capacity of 22,500 MW was completed in 2009, but has displaced more than 1 million people, with some estimates for the final total number reaching above 5 million people, citing official Chinese government sources.

In 2000, the World Commission on Dams estimated the number of people displaced by dams at forty to eighty million globally, compiling secondary data from government sources and academic research. The major dam-building nations China and India alone accounted for twenty-six to fifty-eight million people of this global figure (1950–90), with dam-induced displacement representing 34 per cent of all development-induced displacement in China in that period (including displacement due to urban construction).

(3) Refugee camp establishment is characterized by rapid land-use changes. However, activities by camp inhabitants (e.g. fuelwood gathering, subsistence farming) often constitute productive land use around and within the camp where access and use are permitted. Considering the impacts of socio-economic vulnerability, freedom of movement, and host community relations on refugee camps' natural resource access and dependence is critical for research and effective policy formulation.

By the end of 2020, 82.4 million people had been forcibly displaced by conflict, war and persecution, the highest recorded number since 1990.[7] While approximately 78 per cent of the world's refugees live in urban areas; the remaining 22 per cent live in camps managed by the host country in conjunction with the UNHCR. Camps provide humanitarian relief, critical aid, and essentials of food, water, and shelter for refugees fleeing violence in their home countries and expand rapidly with refugee arrival. On average, refugee camps are established in sparsely populated regions within 50 km of the international border crossed by refugees (Van Den Hoek et al., 2018). As of 2018, the median residence within refugee camps was five years. Although designed to be temporary solutions, many refugee camps operate in a state of *'permanent temporariness'*– populated for years on end but still considered a short-term fix to forced displacement caused by violence and persecution.

We used case analysis for refugee camps in Bangladesh, Uganda, Jordan, and Colombia. These four countries have each received large and recent refugee inflows driven by humanitarian and socio-political crises in neighbouring countries of Myanmar, South Sudan, Syria, and Venezuela, respectively. These countries were the origin (source) countries for two-thirds (13.6 million) of the global refugee population under UNHCR protection as of the end of 2019.[8] For each refugee-hosting country, we explored place-specific environmental changes during periods of high refugee inflow, contextualized these changes in country-specific land-use policies, and analyzed short- and long-term land cover changes around selected refugee camps. Open satellite data, UNHCR-designated camp locations, years of camp establishment and occupation, encamped refugee populations, and camp planning boundaries were used to characterize the environmental impact of each camp. The selection of camp sites and their form of resource delivery is highly varied. The 2018 Global Compact on Refugees (GCR) sought to support countries hosting many refugees through a call for international and equitable responsibility-sharing. However, the top-down approach of global migration governance like the GCR can be restricted by State governments and local social contracts, which may evolve to address natural resource use and access.

(4) Resource rushes are often accompanied by relatively discrete inwards mobility events and abrupt land-use changes for settlement establishment and mineral extraction. Under current resource extraction pathways, such

---

[7] UNHCR Global Trends Report, 2021, www.unhcr.org/flagship-reports/globaltrends/.

[8] UNHCR, 2020. Mid-year Trends. https://www.unhcr.org/en-us/statistics/unhcrstats/5e57d0c57/mid-year-trends-2019.html.

rushes are typically characterized by trade-offs between improved socio-economic outcomes for migrants (and local communities more generally) and widespread environmental externalities.

Although estimates vary, there are thought to be 100 million people directly and indirectly engaged in ASM globally in over eighty countries. Most of these countries are low-income nations in sub-Saharan Africa, South America, Oceania, and Asia. In many of these countries, ASM is a long-established craft that antedates European contact and colonialism, for instance in the Akan region of Ghana, traditional gold mining was used for the kingdom of Akan. Today ASM has been estimated to account for 80 per cent of global sapphire, 20 per cent of gold mining, and up to 20 per cent of diamond extraction. It has become linked to global mineral commodity markets, and is heavily criticized for environmental degradation, linkages to smuggling, labour trafficking, money laundering, and intensifying negative social and ecological externalities. Despite this, ASM has been established as a poverty-driven livelihood strategy that attracts a labour force willing to work under hazardous conditions to supplement low incomes. In developing countries, diminishing agricultural productivity and poverty have been identified as drivers pushing the rural labour force into ASM.

While some empirical literature suggests that abundance of natural resources may fail to improve living standards, or even hinder economic performance, especially in the presence of weak institutions. Most of the evidence, however, comes from aggregate data at the country level and offers little guidance about the local economic effects of resource abundance. In our setting, however, mineral resources might actually provide income in times where agricultural yields dwindle. Thus, there is an internal migratory impact of minerals in the short-term. Through our spatial econometric analysis, we find positive effects of mineral resource presence within a data cell on the sensitivity to Standardized Precipitation Evapotranspiration Index (SPEI) changes. That is, adverse drought effects are dampened by the presence of mineral resources, probably due to the possibility to gain access to an alternative source of income.

(5) Impact of droughts on migration is highly dependent on local income.

Using episodes of drought as an indirect indicator of land resource stress, we find that throughout Africa, internal migration increases with natural resource stress. For the relatively richer countries, drought is also associated with increased international migration. For the poorer countries, drought is associated with decreased international migration, indicating liquidity constraints on this type of mobility (i.e. immobility or 'trapped' populations).

We investigated the impact of drought on migration through an effect on agricultural productivity and, hence, test the hypothesis that communities experiencing larger environmental stress may have suffered declining agricultural productivity leading to mobility. This channel, which should mainly affect rural populations, has differential consequences on emigration rates depending on the income level of potential migrants. In very poor countries, where the main obstacle to migration is that people are not wealthy enough to afford the costs of emigration, warming and lower rural income may imply less emigration. In countries where income is not as low, however, lower agricultural productivity will enhance the incentives to migrate either to cities or abroad. Consistent with this theoretical framework, we find drought episodes to be associated with lower human mobility in low-income environments.

On the other hand, we find that the presence of alternative sources of income greatly improves drought resilience at the national and sub-national level. By combining both international and sub-national models, we are able to extend previous findings on drought resilience by shedding light on the importance of local sources of income other than the drought sensitive agricultural sector. Furthermore, droughts seem to be mostly related with sub-national migration as opposed to international migration decisions. As the latter tend to require larger monetary funds to be even viable, droughts, by their adverse effects on agricultural productivity, cause poverty traps at the national level. Given worsening climate conditions and increased incidences of drought in the future, investment in and development of alternative sources of income seems paramount in alleviating the natural resources related climate stresses in severely affected areas.

(6) Reductions in soil carbon is not significantly related to mobility flows. Quantitative analysis of data sets linking ecological indicators and migration flows in Africa suggest that soil carbon is impacted by a variety of fire ecology factors that mitigate against making any linkage to migration flows.

By analyzing agricultural pathway to migration in more detail, we highlight the mechanism of deteriorating land resources due to drought. In particular, we explore the statistical relationship between the SPEI and both international migration flows and sub-national population densities, and thus internal migration flows. The SPEI is a measure of drought and by extension an indicator of stressed land resources in terms of productivity. We take this examination of land resource degradation further by looking at the influence of soil carbon on migration flows. Finally, we explore whether the presence of mineral resources acts as a mediating factor in the relationship between drought and migration.

Focusing on the African continent due to the expected importance of environmental shocks as a driver of human mobility in this world region in the future, we find that for locations that have a low-income levels, drought conditions are statistically related to increased internal migration from the drought areas. However, at the international level for these countries we find this effect is reversed, with drought being associated with decreased international migration. The magnitude of this drought effect is smaller at the international level than the sub-national. We also find that the longer a location is affected by drought, the stronger this effect is. However, with regards to soil degradation, we find that reductions in soil carbon are not significantly related to migration flows. Lastly, we find that the presence of mineral resources dampens the influence of drought on migration. The reasoning why soil carbon is not significantly related to mobility flows while other variables deserve further research investigation. This may be due to the variable replenishment effects of inorganic and organic sources of carbon entering the soil reservoir. Human charcoal usage and fire ecology can also have confounding influences on soil carbon.

(7) Making systems mapping a part of more policy intervention planning could help visualize trigger points and areas in need of support. Systems maps highlight factors that may act as policy intervention points to reduce the link from natural resource shocks to forced or undesirable (im)mobility (Berry et al., 2018; Hayward & Ayeb-Karlsson, 2021; Orievulu et al., 2020).

When analyzing the linkage between the natural resources and human mobility or immobility three scenarios can be put forward to further our understanding. The first is where the people moving feel forced to move (or unable to move) because of an individual, household or society being detrimentally affected by a degradation or reduction of natural resources available to them. The second is where the process of migration is seen as an adaptation to the loss or potential loss of natural resources. The move in this scenario may not only reduce exposure to resource loss and degradation but also provide income and skills that can be used to build resilience to shocks and stresses. In both of these scenarios natural resources can be seen as conduits of climatic stress and shocks. However, resource degradation and loss can also be a result of non-climatic reasons including poor resource governance. The third scenario is where human mobility is seen as a response to the perceived opportunity provided by natural resources, such as resource mining. Clearly these scenarios are not mutually exclusive, and people can be forced to move while the process of migration still help them adapt. Likewise, populations may choose to migrate to cities for reasons totally unrelated to resource loss, but then be exposed to new risks that are a symptom of resource degradation.

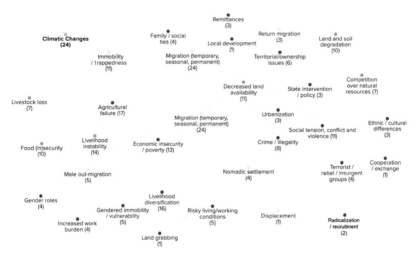

Figure 12 Systems diagram of how migration and immobility relate to natural resource degradation over the Sahel based on a literature review. Green dots represent the environmental impacts, blue ones represent natural resource-based factors, red dots are human and social factors, yellow ones outline the (im)mobility outcomes and finally the purple dot indicates well-being. The numbers indicate how many out of the twenty-four selected journal articles that made this specific link.

Source: Ayeb-Karlsson et al. (2022).

This policy space is based around the aims and assumptions of mobility justice. Human (im)mobility should be based on a rights approach that ensure that people have the right[9] to stay or move to/within their country, and that people should not be discriminated against for being migrants or for deciding to stay in an environmentally risky area. In order to identify the entry points for policies to ensure these aims, we believe that a systems approach can be useful. Systems diagrams illustrate the holistic network linking (im)mobility and natural resources together (Figure 12). In particular, it delves into the many socio-psychological, political, economic, environmental, and demographic (SPEED) factors that often mediate the relationships between resource degradation and human mobility.

(8) Policies within the resource–mobility nexus should be aligned along two fundamental objectives. Firstly, attempting to enhance the possibility of adaptation, greater sustainability of resources, and socio-economic and

---

9 Article 13 of the Universal Declaration of Human Rights from 1948 states that; (1) Everyone has the right to freedom of movement and residence within the borders of each state, and (2) Everyone has the right to leave any country, including his own, and to return to his country. For further details, see www.un.org/en/about-us/universal-declaration-of-human-rights.

environmental resilience so that resource pressures do not *force* people to move; secondly, when this cannot be ensured, promoting safe and well-managed movement of people to other locations.

Using a concept mapping approach, we build trends from ethnographic testimonies from environmentally vulnerable localities into a visual network of how resources and (im)mobility interact on an individual, familial and group level. Here, the links between resources and migration are mediated by a wide variety of socio-psychological, political, economic, and demographic factors, alongside environmental ones. In contrast to policymaking surrounding climate change and socio-economic development targets that fit within sustainability agendas and frameworks, approaches and mechanisms through which to quantify and manage resources are (like associated data points) relatively underdeveloped. Accordingly, there are only a handful of *existing* examples of policies that broach the link between resources and migration. Many of these are, however, embedded within parts of separated approaches to climate change and sustainability, and migration rather than consisting of a holistic policy framework.

Our analysis of policy approaches and interventions that could be used to build a greater practical application of linking resources and migration is split into three areas: preventative policies to address resource constraints at points of origin which can prompt emigration: policies that allow for mobility flow in situations where populations may be trapped due to resource constraints to movement or disasters: and policies that facilitate adaptation at destination points of immigration that have been spurred by resource drivers.

(9) Land ownership and tenure over resources can mitigate forced migration but also allows greater opportunity for voluntary mobility. Property rights to resources can create resilience for populations in times of natural systems stress and prevent involuntary migration. However, such tenure can also provide opportunity for greater mobility and hybrid livelihood situations where one family member may move temporarily for supplemental income.

   – *Strengthening the vitality and sustainability of the resource base.* Approaches that protect and (where possible) restore resources have the potential to stimulate improvements in socio-economic resilience, especially in areas with livelihoods that are strongly tied to natural resources (such as agriculture, fisheries). Resource inventories, combined with land classification and zoning systems could be very valuable ways of quantifying and managing local and regional resources, acting alongside more traditional conservation and restoration approaches.

– *Ensuring local communities have rights of ownership and tenure over resources.* Encouraging security and 'buy in' to resource bases has the capacity to create a much greater vested interest in protecting them. Effective and equitable implementation of common property approaches, such as 'markets' for the likes of water resources, can be utilized in combination with more general land reforms to make livelihoods tied to natural resources more secure.

– *Foster livelihoods that are less directly reliant upon resources.* Diversification of income or livelihood sources can alleviate pressure on resource stocks and reduce population vulnerable to changes in those stocks. A hybridity of income should be facilitated for families whose primary income sources may be seasonal or vulnerable to commodity price fluctuations (such as extractive industries) or security concerns (such as tourism).

– *Facilitate quicker and more reliable relief in disaster events.* Sudden extreme environmental events and their aftermath can dramatically disrupt resources of various kinds and heighten vulnerability for many people in the affected area. Often relief efforts are ad hoc, meaning delays in administering assistance, and targeted on alleviating immediate human concerns rather than livelihoods overall over the longer term. Bolstering dedicated internationally mandated natural hazards funds (like the International Disaster Assistance account), and national and regional 'insurance policies' (like the African Risk Capacity fund) are likely to be able to significantly reduce the number of people 'trapped' in areas of scarce resources and allow movement away from those areas if appropriate.

(10) Remittances of migrants to their home countries can be leveraged for natural resource restoration efforts. The economic value of remittances by migrants to vulnerable resource stressed countries can be an important mechanism to promote policy innovations such as 'green remittance bonds'. A systems approach to considering the positive feedback loops of migration are instantiated by such interventions.

– *Harness support from diaspora that encourages sustainable resource use 'back home'.* Remittances have repeatedly demonstrated a high degree of stability in most countries where their presence is significant in supporting families at home. Initiatives that match incoming remittances are likely to be notable in reducing vulnerability for people left behind (or 'trapped') and alleviate pressures on local resources. There is also the potential to match remittances on the basis of investment in sustainable resource use initiatives.

– *Encourage dialogue and action on effectively planned and orderly resettlements.* The process of proactively approaching the resettlement of people already or potentially significantly affected by declines in resources such as land (for both agricultural and residential use) and potable water has already begun in the case of some small island developing States. An extension of such policies is likely to be needed in other similar contexts of diminishing resources, whether this is a 'managed retreat' of populations away from environmentally vulnerable areas within countries or tactfully managed initiatives for relocation regionally or internationally.

Integrative Lessons

Focusing on the role of natural resources in (im)mobility decisions and outcomes, enables a closer identification of targeted regional, national, and local policy intervention points, than when looking purely at the link between factors like climate change and (im)mobility. Firstly, that (im)mobility should be based on a rights approach, as people having the right[10] to stay or move to/within their country, and that people should not be discriminated against for being migrants or for deciding to stay in an environmentally risky area. Secondly, that the sustainable management of resources provides the platform for people to enjoy this rights-based approach. In a sense the aim of policy in this realm is to try to decouple the degradation of natural resources from (im)mobility. Thirdly to integrate migrants and the process of migration into achieving the sustainable management of resources. In order to identify the entry points for policies to ensure these aims, we have taken a systems approach to illustrate the many processes linking (im)mobility and natural resources. In particular, our analysis delves into the many SPEED factors that have been evidenced and mediate the relationship between resource degradation and human mobility.

In cases where involuntary migration cannot be avoided for a variety of natural and anthropogenic factors, proactively approaching the resettlement process is essential. Such migration of populations affected by declines in resources such as land (for both agricultural and residential use) and potable water has already begun in the case of some small island developing States.

The resource–mobility nexus challenges conventional approaches to policymaking because of its inherent properties as a complex adaptive system. The IRP has thus approached this topic at multiple layers where resource drivers and impacts of human mobility are considered as part of a connected system of

---

[10] See footnote 6.

feedback loops. Since migration can be an adaptive strategy for resource constraints and in some cases an inability to migrate can itself cause greater resource stress, linear models and causal theories for policy impact are elusive. An adaptive planning framework is needed with continuous monitoring of a range of data and thresholds. Policymakers need to be flexible in their decision-making approaches and be informed by some of the planning frameworks that are derived from the computational field of operations research. The policy-planning process in a complex adaptive system is thus inherently iterative. The Appendix provides some specific examples of policy actions that could be developed in this regard. The goal in the context of our resource nexus with mobility can be measured in terms of efficient resource delivery for a specific target of human well-being, which could be measured through a variety of quality-of-life indices. The most ecologically efficient resource consumption patterns that are informed by a separate set of policy decisions can then be mapped to those indicators.

Appendix: Examples of Policy Responses to Migration Emanating from Consultations Conducted during Finalization of IRP Report *Resource Implications of Human Mobility and Migration*

Policy	Impact	Obstacles	Scale	Examples
Microcredit schemes	Ability to obtain assets and capabilities needed to become less susceptible to shocks and stresses and/or cope with their impacts	Repayments can further trap people in place Limited availability. Often resources do not reach poorest of the poor	Usually local	Self-Employed Women's Association (India) Bangladesh Unemployed Rehabilitation Organisation
Natural hazard related financial support	Access rapid and predictable financing when disaster strikes for food security and livelihoods	Usually currently served on an ad hoc basis, meaning delays. Often linked to formalized (exc. informal) economy	Regional to international	
Insurance policies	Expanding the financial resilience of the population to disasters and shocks	Affordability issues, large transaction costs for small portfolios, weak institutions, lack of trust	Local to national	Turkish Catastrophe Insurance Pool. Mongolian Livestock Insurance Pool, African Risk Capacity

Resettlement and assisted migration schemes	Allows orderly and managed movement of people away from already affected or vulnerable areas	Often stringent and arbitrary terms attached to eligibility. Does not reach poorest sections of society. Many may not wish to move	Local to national	Viet Nam – GOV and UNFCCC linked planned relocation schemes to support mobility away from risky locations. SIDS – Facilitation of movement to US, NZ through labour schemes and passport and visa support
Remittance schemes that support sustainable resource management 'back home'	Adds to already significant revenues from remittances sent home by diaspora	Reliance upon external resources may limit indigenous development and cause 'brain drain'	International	Pakistan – money invested by migrants matched by government
Policies to discourage land conversion	Evaluates propensity of soil to be eroded and other soil qualities. Easy to interpret	Lack of baseline data in many country contexts	Local to country scale	United States' Land capability classification system: no subsidies provided for land conversions within certain classes where land degradation is likely

(cont.)

Policy	Impact	Obstacles	Scale	Examples
Land-use planning: common property approach	Gives communities agency over resource use decisions	Corruption: local 'land grabbing' for onward sale. Gender: if only men inherit land based on cultural norms	Country-specific. Need to identify culturally appropriate policies	Bolivia's land reforms: communities needed to organize and given land tenure. Can then decide locally how to utilize land
Resource inventories	Discourage migration to areas of resource vulnerability or scarcity	Lack of baseline data in many country contexts	Local to country scale	USDA's National Resource Inventory: collects and produces information on the status and trends of land, soil, water, and related resources
Land restoration efforts	Inform decisions about where to invest in restoration	Currently largely conceptual. Restoring areas that are likely to be (re) degraded	Local to regional	Africa's Green Wall, Pakistan's Tree Tsunami, Mexico's Forestry Commission
Water markets	Compensate users (farmers) for the use of finite water resources	Sufficiently factoring in 'externalities' into market dynamics	Regional to country	United States Australia Chile China

References

Abbas Khan, K., Zaman, K., Shoukry, A. M. et al. (2019). Natural disasters and economic losses: Controlling external migration, energy and environmental resources, water demand, and financial development for global prosperity. *Environmental Science and Pollution Research*, *26*(14), 14287–14299. https://doi.org/10.1007/s11356-019-04755-5.

Abdul-Rahim, A., Sun, C., & Noraida, A. (2018). The impact of soil and water conservation on agricultural economic growth and rural poverty reduction in China. *Sustainability*, *10*(12), 4444. https://doi.org/10.3390/su10124444.

Adams, R. H. (2007). International remittances and the household: Analysis and review of global evidence. *World Bank Policy Research Working Paper*, *4116*, 32.

Adger, W.N., J.M. Pulhin, J. Barnett, G.D. Dabelko, G.K. Hovelsrud, M. Levy, Ú. Oswald Spring, and C.H. Vogel. (2014). Human security. In Field, C.B., V. R. Barros, D.J. Dokken, K.J. Mach, M.D. Mastrandrea, T.E. Bilir, M. Chatterjee, K.L. Ebi, Y.O. Estrada, R.C. Genova, B. Girma, E.S. Kissel, A.N. Levy, S. MacCracken, P.R. Mastrandrea, and L.L. White (Eds.), *Climate Change 2014: Impacts, Adaptation, and Vulnerability. Part A: Global and Sectoral Aspects. Contribution of Working Group II to the Fifth Assessment Report of the Intergovernmental Panel on Climate Change* (pp. 755–791). Cambridge University Press.

Adger, W. N. (2006). Vulnerability. *Global Environmental Change*, *16*(3), 268–281. https://doi.org/10.1016/j.gloenvcha.2006.02.006.

Adger, W. N., de Campos, R. S., Codjoe, S. N. A. et al. (2021). Perceived environmental risks and insecurity reduce future migration intentions in hazardous migration source areas. *One Earth*, *4*(1), 146–157. https://doi.org/10.1016/j.oneear.2020.12.009.

Afifi, T. (2011). Economic or Environmental Migration? The Push Factors in Niger. International Migration, 49(s1), 95–124. https://doi.org/10.1111/j.1468-2435.2010.00644.x.

Afifi, T., Liwenga, E., & Kwezi, L. (2014). Rainfall-induced crop failure, food insecurity and out-migration in Same-Kilimanjaro, Tanzania. *Climate and Development*, *6*(1), 53–60. https://doi.org/10.1080/17565529.2013.826128.

Ahmed, I., Ayeb-Karlsson, S., van der Geest, K., Huq, S., & Jordan, J. C. (2019). Climate change, environmental stress and loss of livelihoods can push people towards illegal activities: A case study from coastal Bangladesh. *Climate and Development*, *11*(10), 907–917. https://doi.org/10.1080/17565529.2019.1586638.

Albaladejo, J., Díaz-Pereira, E., & de Vente, J. (2021). Eco-holistic soil conservation to support land degradation neutrality and the sustainable development goals. *CATENA*, *196*, 104823. https://doi.org/10.1016/j.catena.2020.104823.

Alden Wily, L. (2018). Risks to the sanctity of community lands in Kenya. A critical assessment of new legislation with reference to forestlands. *Land Use Policy*, *75*, 661–672. https://doi.org/10.1016/j.landusepol.2018.02.006.

Amoah, N., & Stemn, E. (2018). Siting a centralised processing centre for artisanal and small-scale mining – A spatial multi-criteria approach. *Journal of Sustainable Mining*, *17*(4), 215–225. https://doi.org/10.1016/j.jsm.2018.10.001.

Audia, C., Visman, E., Fox, G., Mwangi, E., Kilavi, M., Arango, M., Ayeb-Karlsson, S., & Kniveton, D. (2021). Decision-making heuristics for managing climate-related risks: introducing equity to the FREE framework. In D. Conway & K. Vincent (Eds.), *Climate Risk in Africa: Adaptation and Resilience* (pp. 57–76). Springer International Publishing. https://doi.org/10.1007/978-3-030-61160-6_4.

Ayeb-Karlsson, S., Hayward, G., & Kniveton, D. (forthcoming). A systems analysis of the complex pathways linking natural resources and human (im)mobility in the Sahel region. Working Paper 1.1.

Ayeb-Karlsson, S., Smith, C. D., & Kniveton, D. (2018). A discursive review of the textual use of 'trapped' in environmental migration studies: The conceptual birth and troubled teenage years of trapped populations. *Ambio*, *47*(5), 557–573. https://doi.org/10.1007/s13280-017-1007-6.

Ayeb-Karlsson, S., van der Geest, K., Ahmed, I., Huq, S., & Warner, K. (2016). A people-centred perspective on climate change, environmental stress, and livelihood resilience in Bangladesh. *Sustainability Science*, *11*(4), 679–694. https://doi.org/10.1007/s11625-016-0379-z.

Baldwin, A., Fröhlich, C., & Rothe, D. (2019). From climate migration to anthropocene mobilities: Shifting the debate. *Mobilities*, *14*(3), 289–297. https://doi.org/10.1080/17450101.2019.1620510.

Baldwin, A., Methmann, C., & Rothe, D. (2014). Securitizing 'climate refugees': The futurology of climate-induced migration. *Critical Studies on Security*, *2*(2), 121–130. https://doi.org/10.1080/21624887.2014.943570.

Banerjee, S., Kniveton, D., Black, R. et al. (2017). *Do Financial Remittances Build Household- Level Adaptive Capacity? A Case Study of Flood-Affected Households in India*. KNOMAD WORKING PAPER 18. https://www.knomad.org/sites/default/files/2017-04/KNOMAD%20WP%20Do%20financial%20remittances%20build%20household%20level%20adaptive%20capacity-%20anuary%202017%202017.pdf.

Barrett, C. B., & Bevis, L. E. M. (2015). The self-reinforcing feedback between low soil fertility and chronic poverty. *Nature Geoscience*, *8*(12), 907–912. https://doi.org/10.1038/ngeo2591.

Barnett, J., & O'Neill, S. (2010). Maladaptation. *Global Environmental Change*, *20*(2), 211–213. https://doi.org/10.1016/j.gloenvcha.2009.11.004.

Beine, M., & Parsons, C. (2015). Climatic factors as determinants of international migration. *The Scandinavian Journal of Economics*, *117*(2), 723–767. https://doi.org/10.1111/sjoe.12098.

Berkes, F., Colding, J., & Folke, C. (Eds.). (2002). *Navigating Social-Ecological Systems: Building Resilience for Complexity and Change*. Cambridge University Press. https://doi.org/10.1017/CBO9780511541957.

Bermeo, S. B., & Leblang, D. (2015). Migration and foreign aid. *International Organization*, *69*(3), 627–657. https://doi.org/10.1017/S0020818315000119.

Berry, H. L., Waite, T. D., Dear, K. B. G., Capon, A. G., & Murray, V. (2018). The case for systems thinking about climate change and mental health. *Nature Climate Change*, *8*(4), 282–290. https://doi.org/10.1038/s41558-018-0102-4.

Biermann, F. (2007). 'Earth system governance' as a crosscutting theme of global change research. *Global Environmental Change*, *17* (3–4), 326–337. https://doi.org/10.1016/j.gloenvcha.2006.11.010.

Biermann, F. (2010). Earth system governance and the social sciences. In M. Gross & H. Heinrichs (Eds.), *Environmental Sociology: European Perspectives and Interdisciplinary Challenges* (pp. 59–78). Springer. https://doi.org/10.1007/978-90-481-8730-0_4.

Biermann, F., Abbott, K., Andresen, S. et al. (2012). Navigating the anthropocene: Improving earth system governance. *Science*, *335*(6074), 1306–1307. https://doi.org/10.1126/science.1217255.

Biermann, F., Betsill, M. M., Gupta, J. et al. (2010). Earth system governance: A research framework. *International Environmental Agreements: Politics, Law and Economics*, *10*(4), 277–298. https://doi.org/10.1007/s10784-010-9137-3.

Biermann, F., & Kalfagianni, A. (2020). Planetary justice: A research framework. *Exploring Planetary Justice*, *6*, 100049. https://doi.org/10.1016/j.esg.2020.100049.

Biermann, F., Kanie, N., & Kim, R. E. (2017). Global governance by goal-setting: The novel approach of the UN sustainable development goals. *Open Issue, Part II, 26–27*, 26–31. https://doi.org/10.1016/j.cosust.2017.01.010.

Biermann, F., & Kim, R. E. (Eds.). (2020). *Architectures of Earth System Governance: Institutional Complexity and Structural Transformation* (1st ed.). Cambridge University Press. https://doi.org/10.1017/9781108784641.

Bilsborrow, R. E., & DeLargy, P. F. (1990). Land use, migration, and natural resource deterioration: The experience of Guatemala and the Sudan. *Population and Development Review, 16*, 125–147. https://doi.org/10.2307/2808067.

Biswas, B., & Mallick, B. (2021). Livelihood diversification as key to long-term non-migration: Evidence from coastal Bangladesh. *Environment, Development and Sustainability, 23*(6), 8924–8948. https://doi.org/10.1007/s10668-020-01005-4.

Black, R., Adger, W. N., Arnell, N. W. et al. (2011). The effect of environmental change on human migration. *Global Environmental Change, 21*, S3–S11. https://doi.org/10.1016/j.gloenvcha.2011.10.001.

Black, R., Arnell, N. W., Adger, W. N., Thomas, D., & Geddes, A. (2013). Migration, immobility and displacement outcomes following extreme events. *Environmental Science & Policy, 27*, S32–S43. https://doi.org/10.1016/j.envsci.2012.09.001.

Bohra-Mishra, P., Oppenheimer, M., Cai, R., Feng, S., & Licker, R. (2017). Climate variability and migration in the Philippines. Population and Environment, 38(3), 286–308. Scopus. https://doi.org/10.1007/s11111-016-0263-x.

Borrelli, P., Robinson, D. A., Fleischer, L. R. et al. (2017). An assessment of the global impact of 21st century land use change on soil erosion. *Nature Communications, 8*(1), 2013. https://doi.org/10.1038/s41467-017-02142-7.

Borrelli, P., Robinson, D. A., Panagos, P. et al. (2020). Land use and climate change impacts on global soil erosion by water (2015–2070). *Proceedings of the National Academy of Sciences, 117*(36), 21994–22001. https://doi.org/10.1073/pnas.2001403117.

Brown, O. (2008). *Migration and Climate Change* (IOM Migration Research Series). International Organization for Migration (IOM).

Brown, O., & McLeman, R. (2013). Climate change and migration: An overview. In I. Ness (ed) *The Encyclopedia of Global Human Migration*. Blackwell. https://doi.org/10.1002/9781444351071.wbeghm140.

Burch, S., Gupta, A., Inoue, C. Y. A. et al. (2019). New directions in earth system governance research. *Earth System Governance, 1*, 100006. https://doi.org/10.1016/j.esg.2019.100006.

Burkett, M. (2015). Rehabilitation: A proposal for a climate compensation mechanism for small Island states. *Santa Clara Journal of International Law, 13*(1), 81–124.

Cai, R., Feng, S., Oppenheimer, M., & Pytlikova, M. (2016). Climate variability and international migration: The importance of the agricultural linkage. *Journal of Environmental Economics and Management, 79*, 135–151. https://doi.org/10.1016/j.jeem.2016.06.005.

Carbon Brief. (2017). *Explainer: Dealing with the 'Loss and Damage' Caused by Climate Change*. Carbon Brief. www.carbonbrief.org/explainer-dealing-with-the-loss-and-damage-caused-by-climate-change.

Cardona, O.-D., van Aalst, M. K., Birkmann, J. et al. (2012). Determinants of risk: Exposure and vulnerability. In C. B. Field, V. Barros, T. F. Stocker, & Q. Dahe (Eds.), *Managing the Risks of Extreme Events and Disasters to Advance Climate Change Adaptation* (pp. 65–108). Cambridge University Press. https://doi.org/10.1017/CBO9781139177245.005.

Carey, J. (2020). Core Concept: Managed retreat increasingly seen as necessary in response to climate change's fury. *Proceedings of the National Academy of Sciences*, *117*(24), 13182. https://doi.org/10.1073/pnas.2008198117.

Cattaneo, C., Beine, M., Fröhlich, C. J. et al. (2019). Human migration in the era of climate change. *Review of Environmental Economics and Policy*, *13*(2), 189–206. https://doi.org/10.1093/reep/rez008.

Clifford, M. J. (2014). Future strategies for tackling mercury pollution in the artisanal gold mining sector: Making the minamata convention work. *Futures*, *62*, 106–112. https://doi.org/10.1016/j.futures.2014.05.001.

Dalby, S. (2002). *Environmental Security*. University of Minnesota Press.

de Haas, H. (2010). Migration and development: A theoretical perspective. *International Migration Review*, *44*(1), 227–264. https://doi.org/10.1111/j.1747-7379.2009.00804.x.

De Santo, E. M., Ásgeirsdóttir, Á., Barros-Platiau, A. et al. (2019). Protecting biodiversity in areas beyond national jurisdiction: An earth system governance perspective. *Earth System Governance*, *2*, 100029. https://doi.org/10.1016/j.esg.2019.100029.

Dirth, E., Biermann, F., & Kalfagianni, A. (2020). What do researchers mean when talking about justice? An empirical review of justice narratives in global change research. *Exploring Planetary Justice*, *6*, 100042. https://doi.org/10.1016/j.esg.2020.100042.

Döös, B. R. (1997). Can large-scale environmental migrations be predicted? *Global Environmental Change*, *7*(1), 41–61. https://doi.org/10.1016/S0959-3780(96)00037-4.

Duit, A., Galaz, V., Eckerberg, K., & Ebbesson, J. (2010). Governance, complexity, and resilience. Governance, Complexity and Resilience, 20(3), 363–368. https://doi.org/10.1016/j.gloenvcha.2010.04.006.

Dun, O. (2011). Migration and displacement triggered by floods in the Mekong Delta. *International Migration*, *49* (SUPPL.1), e200–e223. https://doi.org/10.1111/j.1468-2435.2010.00646.x.

Earth Systems Governance. (2022). New Earth Systems Governance Science and Implementation Plan. www.earthsystemgovernance.org/news/new-earth-sys tem-governance-science-and-implementation-plan/. 15 August 2022.

Eriksen, S., Schipper, E. L. F., Scoville-Simonds, M. et al. (2021). Adaptation interventions and their effect on vulnerability in developing countries: Help, hindrance or irrelevance? *World Development*, *141*, 105383. https://doi.org/ 10.1016/j.worlddev.2020.105383.

FAO (Ed.). (2017a). *The Future of Food and Agriculture: Trends and Challenges*. Food and Agriculture Organization of the United Nations.

FAO. (2017b). *Water for Sustainable Food and Agriculture: A Report Produced for the G20 Presidency of Germany*. FAO. www.fao.org/3/i7959e/i7959e .pdf.

Felgentreff, C., & Pott, A. (2016). Climatic turn in migration studies? Geographical perspectives on the relationship between climate and migration. *Erde*, *147*(2), 73–80. https://doi.org/10.12854/erde-147-5.

Feng, S., Krueger, A. B., & Oppenheimer, M. (2010). Linkages among climate change, crop yields and Mexico-US cross-border migration. *Proceedings of the National Academy of Sciences*, *107*(32), 14257–14262. https://doi.org/ 10.1073/pnas.1002632107.

Foresight. (2011). *Foresight: Migration and Global Environmental Change*. UK Government Office for Science, London. https://assets.publishing.ser vice.gov.uk/government/uploads/system/uploads/attachment_data/file/ 287717/11-1116-migration-and-global-environmental-change.pdf.

Gemenne, F., Blocher, J., De Longueville, F. et al. (2017). Climate change, natural disasters and population displacements in West Africa. *Geo-Eco-Trop*, *41*(3), 317–337.

Giampietro, M. (2019). *Multi-Scale Integrated Analysis of Agroecosystems*. CRC PRESS.

Gottlieb, S. (1999). US government to sue tobacco companies. *BMJ*, *319*(7214), 869–869. https://doi.org/10.1136/bmj.319.7214.869.

Gray, C. L. (2011). Soil quality and human migration in Kenya and Uganda. *Global Environmental Change*, *21*(2), 421–430. https://doi.org/10.1016/j .gloenvcha.2011.02.004.

Gray, C., & Wise, E. (2016). Country-specific effects of climate variability on human migration. *Climatic Change*, *135*(3–4), 555–568. https://doi.org/ 10.1007/s10584-015-1592-y.

Greenhill, K. M. (2010). *Weapons of Mass Migration* (1st ed.). Cornell University Press. www.jstor.org.udel.idm.oclc.org/stable/10.7591/j.ctt7v70q.

Gruver, J. B. (2013). *Prediction, Prevention and Remediation of Soil Degradation by Water Erosion | Learn Science at Scitable*. Nature Education Knowledge.

www-nature-com.udel.idm.oclc.org/scitable/knowledge/library/prediction-pre vention-and-remediation-of-soil-degradation–113130829/.

Guadagno, L. (2017). Human mobility in a socio-environmental context: Complex effects on environmental risk. In K. Sudmeier-Rieux, M. Fernández, I. M. Penna, M. Jaboyedoff, & J. C. Gaillard (Eds.), *Identifying Emerging Issues in Disaster Risk Reduction, Migration, Climate Change and Sustainable Development: Shaping Debates and Policies* (pp. 13–31). Springer. https://doi.org/10.1007/978-3-319-33880-4_2.

Gunderson, L. H., & Holling, C. S. (2002). *Panarchy: Understanding Transformations in Human and Natural Systems*. Island Press; WorldCat. org. www.gbv.de/dms/sub-hamburg/349430667.pdf.

Hallegatte, S. (2009). Strategies to adapt to an uncertain climate change. *Traditional Peoples and Climate Change*, *19*(2), 240–247. https://doi.org/10.1016/j.gloenvcha.2008.12.003.

Hamilton, L. C., Colocousis, C. R., & Johansen, S. T. F. (2004). Migration from resource depletion: The case of the Faroe Islands. *Society & Natural Resources*, *17*(5), 443–453. https://doi.org/10.1080/08941920490430232.

Hayward, G., & Ayeb-Karlsson, S. (2021). 'Seeing with empty eyes': A systems approach to understand climate change and mental health in Bangladesh. *Climatic Change*, *165*(1), 29. https://doi.org/10.1007/s10584-021-03053-9.

Herrick, J. E., Abrahamse, T., & United Nations Environment Programme. (2019). *Land Restoration for Achieving the Sustainable Development Goals an International Resource Panel Think Piece*. UNEP, Nairobi, Kenya. https://www.resourcepanel.org/reports/land-restoration-achieving-sustainable-development-goals.

Higgins, D., Balint, T., Liversage, H., & Winters, P. (2018). Investigating the impacts of increased rural land tenure security: A systematic review of the evidence. *Journal of Rural Studies*, *61*, 34–62. https://doi.org/10.1016/j.jrurstud.2018.05.001.

Hilson, G., & Garforth, C. (2012). 'Agricultural poverty' and the expansion of artisanal mining in sub-Saharan Africa: Experiences from Southwest Mali and Southeast Ghana. *Population Research and Policy Review*, *31*(3), 435–464. https://doi.org/10.1007/s11113-012-9229-6.

Hilson, G., & Maponga, O. (2004). How has a shortage of census and geological information impeded the regularization of artisanal and small-scale mining? *Natural Resources Forum*, *28*(1), 22–33. https://doi.org/10.1111/j.0165-0203.2004.00069.x.

Hilson, G., & McQuilken, J. (2014). Four decades of support for artisanal and small-scale mining in sub-Saharan Africa: A critical review. *The Extractive*

Industries and Society, *1*(1), 104–118. https://doi.org/10.1016/j.exis.2014 .01.002.

Huidobro, P., Veiga, M. M., & Adler, S. (2006). *Manual for Training Artisanal and Small-Scale Gold Miners*. GEF/UNDP/UNIDO.

Ian Bryceson & Alfredo Massinga. (2002). Coastal resources and management systems influenced by conflict and migration: Mecúfi, Mozambique. *AMBIO: A Journal of the Human Environment*, *31*(7), 512–517. https://doi.org/ 10.1579/0044-7447-31.7.512.

IBRD, & World Bank. (2006). *Economic Implications of Remittances and Migration*. World Bank.

IGF. (2018). *Global Trends in Artisanal and Small-Scale Mining (ASM): A review of key numbers and issues*. The International Institute for Sustainable Development, Winnipeg, Canada. https://www.iisd.org/system/ files/publications/igf-asm-global-trends.pdf

IOM (2019) *Glossary on Migration*. https://environmentalmigration.iom.int/ sites/g/files/tmzbdl1411/files/iml_34_glossary.pdf

International Organization for Migration and World Food Programme (2022). *Understanding the adverse drivers and implications of migration from El Salvador, Guatemala and Honduras*. https://publications.iom.int/books/ understanding-adverse-drivers-and-implications-migration-el-salvador-gua temala-and-honduras.

Ionesco, D., Mokhnacheva, D., & Gemenne, F. (2017). *The Atlas of Environmental Migration* (1st ed.). Routledge. https://doi.org/10.4324/9781 315777313.

Johnson, S. (19 August 2019). Expatriate workers' remittances targeted as source of finance. *Financial Times*. www.ft.com/content/6cfd7b78-b92f-11e9-8a88-aa6628ac896c.

Juhola, S., Glaas, E., Linnér, B.-O., & Neset, T.-S. (2016). Redefining maladaptation. *Environmental Science & Policy*, *55*, 135–140. https://doi .org/10.1016/j.envsci.2015.09.014.

Kashwan, P., Biermann, F., Gupta, A., & Okereke, C. (2020). Planetary justice: Prioritizing the poor in earth system governance. *Exploring Planetary Justice*, *6*, 100075. https://doi.org/10.1016/j.esg.2020.100075.

Kassam, A., Derpsch, R., & Friedrich, T. (2014). Global achievements in soil and water conservation: The case of conservation agriculture. *International Soil and Water Conservation Research*, *2*(1), 5–13. https://doi.org/10.1016/ S2095-6339(15)30009-5.

Keesstra, S. D., Bouma, J., Wallinga, J. et al. (2016). The significance of soils and soil science towards realization of the United Nations sustainable development goals. *SOIL*, *2*(2), 111–128. https://doi.org/10.5194/soil-2-111-2016.

Kniveton, D. R., Smith, C. D., & Black, R. (2012). Emerging migration flows in a changing climate in dryland Africa. *Nature Climate Change*, *2*(6), 444–447. https://doi.org/10.1038/nclimate1447.

Kniveton, D., Schmidt-Verkerk, K., Smith, C., & Black, R. (2008). *Climate Change and Migration: Improving Methodologies to Estimate Flows* IOM Migration Research Series, 33. IOM, Switzerland. https://doi.org/10.18356/6233a4b6-en.

Kotzé, L. J., Kim, R. E., Blanchard, C. et al. (2022). Earth system law: Exploring new frontiers in legal science. *Earth System Governance*, *11*, 100126. https://doi.org/10.1016/j.esg.2021.100126.

Kraly, E. P., & Hovy, B. (2020). Data and research to inform global policy: The global compact for safe, orderly and regular migration. *Comparative Migration Studies*, *8*(1), 11. https://doi.org/10.1186/s40878-019-0166-y.

Lanati, M., & Thiele, R. (2018). The impact of foreign aid on migration revisited. *World Development*, *111*, 59–74. https://doi.org/10.1016/j.worlddev.2018.06.021.

Levitt, P. (1998). Social remittances: Migration driven local-level forms of cultural diffusion. *The International Migration Review*, *32*(4), 926–948. https://doi.org/10.2307/2547666.

Ma, X., Heerink, N., Feng, S., & Shi, X. (2015). Farmland tenure in China: Comparing legal, actual and perceived security. *Land Use Policy*, *42*, 293–306. https://doi.org/10.1016/j.landusepol.2014.07.020,

Mace, M. J., & Verheyen, R. (2016). Loss, damage and responsibility after COP21: All options open for the Paris agreement. *Review of European, Comparative & International Environmental Law*, *25*(2), 197–214. https://doi.org/10.1111/reel.12172.

Maclin, B. J., Kelly, J. T. D., Perks, R., Vinck, P., & Pham, P. (2017). Moving to the mines: Motivations of men and women for migration to artisanal and small-scale mining sites in Eastern democratic republic of the Congo. *Resources Policy*, *51*, 115–122. https://doi.org/10.1016/j.resourpol.2016.12.003.

Magnan, A., & Mainguy, G. (2014). Avoiding maladaptation to climate change: Towards guiding principles. *S.A.P.I.EN.S. Surveys and Perspectives Integrating Environment and Society, 7.1*, Article 7.1: 1–11 http://journals.openedition.org/sapiens/1680.

Magnan, A. K., Schipper, E. L. F., Burkett, M. et al. (2016). Addressing the risk of maladaptation to climate change. *WIREs Climate Change*, *7*(5), 646–665. https://doi.org/10.1002/wcc.409.

Makhetha, E. (2020). Artisanal miners, migration and remittances in Southern Africa. In I. Moyo, C. C. Nshimbi, & J. P. Laine (Eds.), *Migration*

Conundrums, Regional Integration and Development: Africa-Europe Relations in a Changing Global Order (pp. 257–270). Springer. https://doi .org/10.1007/978-981-15-2478-3_11.

Mayumi, K., & Giampietro, M. (2006). The epistemological challenge of self-modifying systems: Governance and sustainability in the post-normal science era. *Ecological Economics, 57*(3), 382–399. https://doi.org/10.1016/ j.ecolecon.2005.04.023.

Mbonile, M. J. (2005). Migration and intensification of water conflicts in the Pangani Basin, Tanzania. *Habitat International, 29*(1), 41–67. https://doi .org/10.1016/S0197-3975(03)00061-4.

McAdam, J. (2009). Environmental migration governance. *UNSW Law Research Paper No. 2009-1*: 34pp. https://doi.org/10.2139/ssrn.1412002.

McAdam, J. (2019). The global compacts on refugees and migration: A new era for international protection? *International Journal of Refugee Law, 30*(4), 571–574. https://doi.org/10.1093/ijrl/eez004.

McDaniels, J., Chouinard, R., & Veiga, M. M. (2010). Appraising the global mercury project: An adaptive management approach to combating mercury pollution in small-scale gold mining. *International Journal of Environment and Pollution, 41*(3/4), 242. https://doi.org/10.1504/IJEP.2010.033234.

McLeman, R., & Gemenne, F. (2018). Environmental migration research: Evolution and current state of the science. Chapter 1 In R. McLeman & F. Gemenne (eds.) *Routledge Handbook of Environmental Displacement and Migration.* Routledge.

McLeman, R., Opatowski, M., Borova, B., & Walton-Roberts, M. (2016). Environmental migration and displacement: What we know and don't know (p. 28). Wilfred Laurier University. http://www.laurierenvironmental migration.com/wp-content/uploads/2015/11/WLU-Environmental-Migration-Background-Report.pdf.

Morris, R. (2012). *Scoping Study: Impact of Fly-in Fly-out/Drive-in Drive-out Work Practices on Local Government.* Australian Centre of Excellence for Local Government, University of Technology, Sydney. https://www.uts.edu.au/sites/ default/files/1336624408_ACELG_Scoping_Study_FIFO_May_2012.pdf.

Mullan, K., Grosjean, P., & Kontoleon, A. (2011). Land tenure arrangements and rural–urban migration in China. *World Development, 39*(1), 123–133. https://doi.org/10.1016/j.worlddev.2010.08.009.

Nawrotzki, R. J., Runfola, D. M., Hunter, L. M., & Riosmena, F. (2016). Domestic and international climate migration from rural Mexico. *Human Ecology, 44*(6), 687–699. https://doi.org/10.1007/s10745-016-9859-0.

Nicholson, C. T. M. (2014). Climate change and the politics of causal reasoning: The case of climate change and migration: Climate change and the politics of causal reasoning. *The Geographical Journal*, *180*(2), 151–160. https://doi .org/10.1111/geoj.12062.

Nishimura, L. (2015). 'Climate change migrants': Impediments to a protection framework and the need to incorporate migration into climate change adaptation strategies. *International Journal of Refugee Law*, *27*(1), 107–134. Scopus. https://doi.org/10.1093/ijrl/eev002.

Nyame, F. K., Andrew Grant, J., & Yakovleva, N. (2009). Perspectives on migration patterns in Ghana's mining industry. *Small-Scale Mining, Poverty and Development in Sub-Saharan Africa*, *34*(1), 6–11. https://doi .org/10.1016/j.resourpol.2008.05.005.

Nyantakyi-Frimpong, H., & Bezner Kerr, R. (2017). Land grabbing, social differentiation, intensified migration and food security in northern Ghana. *The Journal of Peasant Studies*, *44*(2), 421–444. https://doi.org/10.1080/ 03066150.2016.1228629.

Obokata, R., Veronis, L., & McLeman, R. (2014). Empirical research on international environmental migration: A systematic review. *Population and Environment*, *36*(1), 111–135. https://doi.org/10.1007/s11111-014-0210-7.

OECD. (2010). *Sustainable Management of Water Resources in Agriculture*. OECD. https://doi.org/10.1787/9789264083578-en.

Orievulu, K., Ayeb-Karlsson, S., Ngema, S. et al. (2020). *Exploring linkages between drought and HIV treatment adherence in Africa: A Systematic Review* [Preprint]. HIV/AIDS. https://doi.org/10.1101/2020.09.03.20187591.

Pachauri, R. K., Mayer, L., & Intergovernmental Panel on Climate Change (Eds.). (2015). *Climate Change 2014: Synthesis Report*. Intergovernmental Panel on Climate Change.

Pierre-Nathoniel, D., Siegele, L., Roper, L.-A., & Menke, I. (2019). *Loss and Damage at COP25: A Hard Fought Step in the Right Direction*. Climate Analytics Blog. https://climateanalytics.org/blog/2019/loss-and-damage-at-cop25-a-hard-fought-step-in-the-right-direction/.

Piguet, E. (2010). Linking climate change, environmental degradation, and migration: A methodological overview. *WIREs Climate Change*, *1*(4), 517–524. https://doi.org/10.1002/wcc.54.

Piguet, E. (2021). Linking climate change, environmental degradation, and migration: An update after 10 years. *Wiley Interdisciplinary Reviews: Climate Change*, 13(1), e746. https://doi.org/10.1002/wcc.746.

Preiser, R., Biggs, R., De Vos, A., & Folke, C. (2018). Social-ecological systems as complex adaptive systems: Organizing principles for advancing research methods and approaches. *Ecology and Society*, *23*(4), art46. https:// doi.org/10.5751/ES-10558-230446.

Rahman, H. M. T., & Hickey, G. M. (2020). An analytical framework for assessing context-specific rural livelihood vulnerability. *Sustainability, 12* (14), 5654. https://doi.org/10.3390/su12145654.

Ramalingam, B. (2013). *Aid on the Edge of Chaos: Rethinking International Cooperation in a Complex World* (1st ed.). Oxford University Press.

Rammel, C., Stagl, S., & Wilfing, H. (2007). Managing complex adaptive systems —A co-evolutionary perspective on natural resource management. *Ecological Economics, 63*(1), 9–21. https://doi.org/10.1016/j.ecolecon.2006.12.014.

Renaud, F. G., Dun, O., Warner, K., & Bogardi, J. (2011). A decision framework for environmentally induced migration. *International Migration, 49*(s1), e5– e29. https://doi.org/10.1111/j.1468-2435.2010.00678.x.

Rigaud, K. K., de Sherbinin, A., Jones, B. et al. (2018). *Groundswell: Preparing for Internal Climate Migration*. World Bank. https://doi.org/ 10.1596/29461.

Roberts, E., & Andrei, S. (2015). The rising tide: Migration as a response to loss and damage from sea level rise in vulnerable communities. *International Journal of Global Warming, 8*(2), 258. https://doi.org/10.1504/ IJGW.2015.071965.

Salerno, J., Mwalyoyo, J., Caro, T., Fitzherbert, E., & Mulder, M. B. (2017). The consequences of internal migration in sub-Saharan Africa: A case study. *BioScience, 67*(7), 664–671. https://doi.org/10.1093/biosci/bix041.

Salerno, J. D., Mulder, M. B., & Kefauver, S. C. (2014). Human migration, protected areas, and conservation outreach in Tanzania: Human migration and protected areas. *Conservation Biology, 28*(3), 841–850. https://doi.org/ 10.1111/cobi.12237.

Sardadvar, S., & Vakulenko, E. (2017). A model of interregional migration under the presence of natural resources: Theory and evidence from Russia. *The Annals of Regional Science, 59*(2), 535–569. https://doi.org/10.1007/ s00168-017-0844-3.

Schade, J. (2016). Land matters: The role of land policies and laws for environmental migration in Kenya. *Migration, Environment and Climate Change: Policy Brief Series 1*(2), Jan. 2016. https://environmentalmigration.iom.int/ sites/g/files/tmzbdl1411/files/documents/policy_brief_issue1.pdf.

Scherr, S., & Yadav, S. (1996). *Land Degradation in the Developing World: Implications for Food, Agriculture, and the Environment to 2*020 (p. 42). International Food Policy Research Institute. https://pdf.usaid.gov/pdf_docs/ pnaby622.pdf.

Schipper, E. L. F. (2020). Maladaptation: When adaptation to climate change goes very wrong. *One Earth, 3*(4), 409–414. https://doi.org/10.1016/j.oneear .2020.09.014.

Sheller, M. (2018). *Mobility Justice: The Politics of Movement in the Age of Extremes*. Verso.

Sheller, M. (2020). *Mobility Justice: The Politics of Movement in an Age of Extremes*. Verso.

Siebenhüner, B., Djalante, R., Jager, N. W., & King, J. P. (2021). Adaptiveness in earth system governance: Synthesis, policy relevance, and the way forward. In B. Siebenhüner & R. Djalante (Eds.), *Adaptiveness: Changing Earth System Governance* (pp. 188–200). Cambridge University Press. https://doi.org/10.1017/9781108782180.012.

Simbizi, M. C. D., Bennett, R. M., & Zevenbergen, J. (2014). Land tenure security: Revisiting and refining the concept for sub-Saharan Africa's rural poor. *Land Use Policy*, *36*, 231–238. https://doi.org/10.1016/j.landusepol.2013.08.006.

Telmer, K. H., & Veiga, M. M. (2009). World emissions of mercury from artisanal and small scale gold mining. In R. Mason & N. Pirrone (Eds.), *Mercury Fate and Transport in the Global Atmosphere: Emissions, Measurements and Models* (pp. 131–172). Springer. https://doi.org/10.1007/978-0-387-93958-2_6.

Tseng, T.-W. J., Robinson, B. E., Bellemare, M. F. et al. (2020). Influence of land tenure interventions on human well-being and environmental outcomes. *Nature Sustainability*, *4*: 242–251 https://doi.org/10.1038/s41893-020-00648-5.

UNCCD. (2014). *Land-based adaptation and Resilience: Powered by Nature*. UNCCD. www.eld-initiative.org/fileadmin/pdf/Land_Based_Adaptation_ENG_Sall_web.pdf.

UNDRR. (2022). Chart of the Sendai Framework for Disaster Risk Reduction 2015–2030. www.preventionweb.net/files/44983_sendaiframeworkchart.pdf. 15 August 2022.

UNFCCC. (2021). *Approaches to Address Loss and Damage associated with Climate Change Impacts in Developing Countries*. UNFCCC. https://unfccc.int/topics/adaptation-and-resilience/workstreams/approaches-to-address-loss-and-damage-associated-with-climate-change-impacts-in-developing-countries#eq-4.

United Nations (Ed.). (2016). *Climate Change Resilience: An Opportunity for Reducing Inequalities*. United Nations.

Upadhyay, H., Kelman, I., Lingaraj, G. J. et al. (2015). Conceptualizing and contextualizing research and policy for links between climate change and migration. *International Journal of Climate Change Strategies and Management*, *7*(3), 394–417. https://doi.org/10.1108/IJCCSM-05-2014-0058.

van den Hoek, R., Murillo-Sandoval, P., Landon Crumley, R., Devenish, A., Fein, F., Kennedy, R.E., Ichien, S., Wrathall, D. & Harris, T. (2018). Refugee Camps as Climate Traps: Measuring the Enviro-climatic Marginality of 922 Global Refugee Camps with Satellite Time Series Data. American

Geophysical Union, Fall Meeting, December 2018. https://ui.adsabs.harvard.edu/abs/2018AGUFMIN44A..04V/abstract.

van der Hel, S., & Biermann, F. (2017). The authority of science in sustainability governance: A structured comparison of six science institutions engaged with the sustainable development goals. *Environmental Science & Policy, 77*, 211–220. https://doi.org/10.1016/j.envsci.2017.03.008.

van der Vliet, J., & Biermann, F. (2022). Global governance of climate migrants: A critical evaluation of the global compacts. In A. Kent & S. Behrman (Eds.), *Climate Refugees: Global, Local and Critical Approaches* (pp. 60–82). Cambridge University Press. https://doi.org/10.1017/9781108902991.004.

Van Praag, L., & Timmerman, C. (2019). Environmental migration and displacement: A new theoretical framework for the study of migration aspirations in response to environmental changes. *Environmental Sociology, 5*(4), 352–361. https://doi.org/10.1080/23251042.2019.1613030.

Vigil, S. (2018). Green grabbing-induced displacement. In R. McLeman & F. Gemenne (Eds.), *Routledge Handbook of Environmental Displacement and Migration* (1st ed., pp. 370–387). Routledge. https://doi.org/10.4324/9781315638843-29.

Vlassopoulos, C. A. (2013). Defining environmental migration in the climate change era: Problem, consequence or solution? In T. Faist & J. Schade (Eds.), *Disentangling Migration and Climate Change* (pp. 145–163). Springer. https://doi.org/10.1007/978-94-007-6208-4_6.

Wewerinke-Singh, M., & Salili, D. H. (2020). Between negotiations and litigation: Vanuatu's perspective on loss and damage from climate change. *Climate Policy, 20*(6), 681–692. https://doi.org/10.1080/14693062.2019.1623166.

Wiek, A., & Walter, A. I. (2009). A transdisciplinary approach for formalized integrated planning and decision-making in complex systems. *European Journal of Operational Research, 197*(1), 360–370. https://doi.org/10.1016/j.ejor.2008.06.013.

Wilson, J. (2020). *Temporary Protected Status: Overview and Current Issues.* Congressional Research Service, p. 21. https://fas.org/sgp/crs/homesec/RS20844.pdf.

Zhang, H., Yan, W., Oba, A., & Zhang, W. (2014). Radiation-driven migration: The case of Minamisoma City, Fukushima, Japan, after the Fukushima nuclear accident. *International Journal of Environmental Research and Public Health, 11*(9), 9286–9305. https://doi.org/10.3390/ijerph110909286.

Zickgraf, C. (2019). Keeping people in place: Political factors of (im)mobility and climate change. *Social Sciences, 8*(8), 228. https://doi.org/10.3390/socsci8080228.

About the Authors

Saleem H. Ali is Blue and Gold Distinguished Professor of Geography at the University of Delaware (USA). He is also a member of the United Nations International Resource Panel and serves on the board of directors of Mediators Beyond Borders International (MBBI). Twitter @saleem_ali

Martin Clifford is a postdoctoral scholar in the Department of Geography and Spatial Sciences at the University of Delaware (USA). He also serves on the Associate Editor of the journal *Extractive Industries and Society.*

Dominic Kniveton is Professor of Climate Change and Society at the University of Sussex. He is a member of the United Nations International Resource Panel and the Lancet Countdown. His work in migration and climate change was recognised with the Royal Geographical Society's Cuthbert Peek award.

Dr. Caroline Zickgraf acts as Deputy Director of the Hugo Observatory: Environment, Migration, Politics in the Department of Geography at the University of Liège in Belgium. She is also the lead governance researcher on the Belmont Forum's project on migration, transformation, and sustainability.

Dr. Sonja Ayeb-Karlsson is a senior researcher and lecturer at the Institute for Risk and Disaster Reduction, University College London (UCL) and the United Nations University's Institute for Environment and Human Security (UNU-EHS). Her research is broad and interdisciplinary with a particular focus on the interconnections between intersectionality, policy and climate change, and their overlaps with human (im)mobility and migration, health and mental well-being or structural violence. Dr. Ayeb-Karlsson leads UCL's Everyday Disasters and Violences Research Group and directs the mental health work of the Lancet Countdown. Her work is well-published and widely covered by media outlets across the world.

Cambridge Elements ≡

Earth System Governance

Frank Biermann
Utrecht University

Frank Biermann is Research Professor of Global Sustainability Governance with the Copernicus Institute of Sustainable Development, Utrecht University, the Netherlands. He is the founding Chair of the Earth System Governance Project, a global transdisciplinary research network launched in 2009; and Editor-in-Chief of the new peer-reviewed journal *Earth System Governance* (Elsevier). In April 2018, he won a European Research Council Advanced Grant for a research programme on the steering effects of the Sustainable Development Goals.

Aarti Gupta
Wageningen University

Aarti Gupta is Professor of Global Environmental Governance at Wageningen University, the Netherlands. She is Lead Faculty and a member of the Scientific Steering Committee of the Earth System Governance (ESG) Project and a Coordinating Lead Author of its 2018 Science and Implementation Plan. She is also principal investigator of the Dutch Research Council-funded TRANSGOV project on the Transformative Potential of Transparency in Climate Governance. She holds a PhD from Yale University in environmental studies.

Michael Mason
London School of Economics and Political Science (LSE)

Michael Mason is Associate Professor in the Department of Geography and Environment at the London School of Economics and Political Science (LSE). At LSE he also Director of the Middle East Centre and an Associate of the Grantham Institute on Climate Change and the Environment. Alongside his academic research on environmental politics and governance, he has advised various governments and international organisations on environmental policy issues, including the European Commission, ICRC, NATO, the UK Government (FCDO) and UNDP.

About the Series

Linked with the Earth System Governance Project, this exciting new series will provide concise but authoritative studies of the governance of complex socio-ecological systems, written by world-leading scholars. Highly interdisciplinary in scope, the series will address governance processes and institutions at all levels of decision-making, from local to global, within a planetary perspective that seeks to align current institutions and governance systems with the fundamental 21st Century challenges of global environmental change and earth system transformations.

Elements in this series will present cutting edge scientific research, while also seeking to contribute innovative transformative ideas towards better governance. A key aim of the series is to present policy-relevant research that is of interest to both academics and policymakers working on earth system governance.

More information about the Earth System Governance project can be found at: www.earthsystemgovernance.org

Cambridge Elements ☰

Earth System Governance

Printed in the United States
by Baker & Taylor Publisher Services